PROCEEDINGS OF THE BRITISH ACADEMY · 102

EDUCATIONAL STANDARDS

Edited by
HARVEY GOLDSTEIN & ANTHONY HEATH

Published for THE BRITISH ACADEMY
by OXFORD UNIVERSITY PRESS

Oxford University Press, Great Clarendon Street, Oxford OX2 6DP

Oxford New York
Athens Auckland Bangkok Bogota Bombay
Buenos Aires Calcutta Cape Town Dar es Salaam
Delhi Florence Hong Kong Istanbul Karachi
Kuala Lumpur Madras Madrid Melbourne
Mexico City Nairobi Paris Singapore
Taipei Tokyo Toronto Warsaw

and associated companies in
Berlin Ibadan

Published in the United States by
Oxford University Press Inc., New York

British Library Cataloguing in Publication Data
Data available

ISBN 0-19-726211-2
ISBN 0-19-726214-7 (Pbk)
ISSN 0068-1202

Typeset by J&L Composition Ltd, Filey, North Yorkshire
Printed in Great Britain
on acid-free paper by
Creative Print and Design Wales
Ebbw Vale

Contents

Notes on Contributors

Richard Aldrich is professor and head of the History and Philosophy Group, Institute of Education, University of London, past president of the International Standing Conference for the History of Education, and an associate editor for the *New DNB*. Recent publications arising from his research in educational policy-making and biography include *Education for the Nation* (1996), *Biographical Dictionary of North American and European Educationists* (1997 with Peter Gordon) and *The National Curriculum beyond 2000* (1998 with John White).

David Bartholomew is Emeritus Professor of Statistics at the London School of Economics which he first joined in 1973 having previously been Professor of Statistics at the University of Kent. He is a former Pro-Director of the LSE and President of the Royal Statistical Society. His main interest is in the application of statistical ideas in the social sciences especially the development of latent variable methods. His latest book is *The Statistical Approach to Social Measurement* (Academic Press, 1996).

Mike Cresswell has been actively engaged in research in educational assessment for over 20 years and is Head of Research and Statistics at the Associated Examining Board. His current research concerns the nature of examination standards and methods for defining, setting, maintaining and studying them. He also has long-standing interests in marker reliability and the problems of combining and equating scores from instruments which differ in difficulty and type. A recent publication is: 'Defining, Setting and Maintaining Standards in Curriculum Embedded Examinations: Judgemental and Statistical Approaches', in H. Goldstein and T. Lewis *Assessment: Problems, Developments and Statistical Issues* (London, Wiley, 1996).

Harvey Goldstein is a Fellow of the British Academy, and Professor of Statistical Methods at the Institute of Education, University of London. His principal research interests lie in the development of statistical methodology for the analysis of complex hierarchical data and the quantitative aspects of educational assessment. He is particularly

interested in the theoretical assumptions implicit in making comparisons of achievement across time and space. A major publication in this
area is the monograph *Interpreting international comparisons of student
achievement* (Paris, UNESCO, 1995).

John Gray has been professor and Director of Research at Homerton
College, Cambridge since 1994 and a Visiting Professor at the London
University Institute of Education. He has researched extensively on
issues to do with school effectiveness, school improvement and the
quality of schooling. He has recently completed a major study funded
by the ESRC of schools which have been improving in effectiveness over
time. Recent books are: *'Good School, Bad School': Evaluating Performance and Encouraging Improvement* and *Improving Schools: Performance
and Potential* (both published by the Open University Press).

A. H. (Chelly) Halsey is a Fellow of the British Academy, emeritus
professor of sociology at the University of Oxford and emeritus fellow
of Nuffield College. His recent books are *Education*, (OUP 1996, with
P. Brown and H. Lauder), *No Discouragement: an autobiography*,
Macmillan, 1996 and *The Decline of Donnish Dominion*, (OUP, 2nd
edition, 1995, and he is currently editing *Twentieth Century British
Social Trends*, Macmillan, (forthcoming).

Anthony Heath is a Fellow of the British Academy, Professor of Sociology at the University of Oxford and professorial fellow at Nuffield
College. He has worked on sociological aspects of educational attainment, particularly on the role of social class differences. His publications include *Origins and Destinations: Family, Class and Education in
Modern Britain* (with A. H. Halsey and J. M. Ridge, 1980), *Sociology
and Social Reform* (ed. with Colin Crouch, 1992), and *Ireland North and
South: Perspectives from the Social Sciences* (ed, with Richard Breen
and Chris Whelan, 1999).

Lindsay Paterson is professor of educational policy at Edinburgh
University. His research is mainly in the area of quantitative sociology.
He has written on many aspects of the sociology of education—in
particular on the effects of social disadvantage and on the expansion
of higher education—and he has written widely on Scottish politics and
culture.

Ian Plewis is a Senior Lecturer in Statistics at the Institute of Education and a Senior Research Officer in the Centre for Longitudinal Studies, Institute of Education. His research interests are in the design and analysis of longitudinal studies, multilevel modelling and educational inequalities. He is the author of *Statistics in Education* (Arnold,1997).

S. J. Prais is a Fellow of the British Academy and senior fellow at the National institute of Economic and Social Research, London, where he has been responsible for an extensive series of international comparisons of productivity, education and training. Since 1993 his team has co-operated with schools an the London borough of Barking and Dagenham in introducing reforms in mathematics teaching.

David Reynolds is Professor of Education at the University of Newcastle upon Tyne. He has researched and published in the areas of school effectiveness, school improvement and educational policy, and his current research interests include mathematics education and international differences in educational achievement. His most recent publication is *The International Handbook of School Effectiveness Research* (Falmer, with Charles Teddlie).

Gillian Sutherland is Fellow, Gwatkin Lecturer and Director of Studies in History, Newnham College, Cambridge. She has written extensively on the social and political history of education in the nineteenth and twentieth century. She is currently working on a double biography of A. J. and B. A. Clough.

Julia Whitburn is a Senior Research Officer at the National Institute of Economic and Social Research and her particular interests are Japanese, Swiss and German education. She has 20 years experience of mathematics teaching and is currently engaged in comparative research into the acquisition of mathematical skills in the early years of schooling. She is also a qualified Ofsted Inspector (Secondary, Primary and Early Years).

Alison Wolf is Professor of Education at the Institute of Education, University of London and Executive Director of its International Centre for Research on Assessment. Her major research interests are vocational, technical and professional assessment and mathematics for post-compulsory non-specialists, in the UK and in comparative contexts. She is the author of *Competency-Based Assessment* (Open University Press), and co-author with Andy Green and Tom Leney of *Convergence and Divergence in European Education and Training Systems* (Institute of Education).

Introduction

HARVEY GOLDSTEIN & ANTHONY HEATH

EDUCATIONAL STANDARDS HAVE FIGURED PROMINENTLY in recent debates over educational policy in the UK and elsewhere. Despite this, or even perhaps because of it, there is little clarity about the nature of a 'standard', little understanding of how such debates are situated historically, and scant awareness of measurement issues. The British Academy invited a number of distinguished academics and researchers to present papers at a one day symposium designed to bring together a number of perspectives on this issue. This symposium was held on 9 October 1998 and a list of participants is given in the appendix. The speakers and discussants were chosen for their expertise in a number of relevant areas, together with an audience which contained other academics and researchers as well as policy makers.

None of the contributors claims to offer a straightforward 'solution' to the problems of definition and measurement, or to be able to provide prescriptions for official policy. Rather, they have attempted to provide an analysis of the nature of the problems and a contextualisation of the debates, both historically and cross-nationally. In this way we hope better to inform public debate. We believe that this is the first serious attempt to bring together such a distinguished collection of scholars on this topic, at least in the UK, and we would recommend these contributions to academics and policy makers alike.

In the first section of the volume Alison Wolf addresses the issue of how far there is an international consensus about the way in which educational standards should operate. She points to important differences between countries. In the USA, for example, the SAT and GRE have become enormously important high-stakes tests for young people

Proceedings of the British Academy, **102**, 1–8. © The British Academy 2000.

seeking entry to higher education courses. They are standardised tests in the sense of machine-readable multiple-choice items, selected on the basis of psychometric criteria. Judgements about content and item format, and therefore what a given level of success actually involves or means are buried from sight. The 'scientific' basis of the test construction seems to be associated with a high level of public confidence in the objectivity of the tests. But unlike the case in Britain comparability over time is not an issue since the function of these high-stakes tests is so overwhelmingly one of ranking and selection. The main preoccupation is not with ensuring that tests and items are equally difficult in some absolute sense, but on the 'objective' rank ordering of individuals.

In contrast to the US, as Wolf points out, 'The Chinese commitment is less to the idea of standards as a measuring tool than to standards as an example and ideal'. No claims are made about substantive achievement levels or their comparability over time. Each examination is a grading system for the candidates, for example in connection with university selection, and the only relevant issue is whether the examination treats a given year's entry fairly. There appears to be an assumption that fairness is achieved by the fact that everyone is confronted by the same assessment. France is rather like China, and has centralised national examinations, the baccalaureat for example, which are very important for certification and selection purposes.

In Sweden, on the other hand, it is teachers with whom a final judgement about candidates is lodged. Consistency is an issue, but it is assumed that teachers can make such judgements so that comparability between schools and across time is maintained. There is, however, some moderation which takes place in grades 8 and 9 whereby national tests results are used to guide teachers in their own judgements. Germany has many elements of the Swedish system with teachers having a final judgement via internal marking of examinations and in many cases responsibility for setting the examinations according to State criteria.

The UK is thus rather unusual internationally in its historical concern with maintaining standards over time as well as across different curriculum subjects, and in the primacy of criterion-related concerns over norm-referencing practices. Public policy pronouncements have recently even incorporated commitments to specific test targets for future years.

Finally Wolf points out that ultimately there is no real escape from having to rely upon professional judgements in attempts to describe and maintain 'standards', and this involves some degree of trust in those professionals. This is a persistent theme throughout the contributions to this volume. In the discussion of Wolf's paper this is emphasised by Reynolds, who also suggests that increased competition between schools may lead to the undermining of such trust. Whitburn notes how different systems vary in the extent to which they carry out centralised testing of all children, Britain being especially notable for the large amount that is carried out. She asks what the purpose of all this testing is, and whether the purposes might not be better achieved by other means. She points out that some tests are now being used primarily to make comparisons between schools and teachers and asks why it is that in England our obsession is with comparing *school* performance? 'Does it reflect our *mistrust* of our schools and our teachers which has been fuelled by those in influential positions? Or is it more a reflection of our unwillingness to attribute individual responsibility for achievement (or failure)? In Japan, there is a widespread belief in the importance of effort rather than innate ability and *pupils* are encouraged to believe that 'If you work hard enough and persevere, you can succeed.' In England the message is that *teachers* need to work harder and persevere in order for their pupils to succeed and where pupils do not achieve well, it is poor teaching that is held to be responsible.'

Aldrich begins his historical review by considering the various definitions and understandings that have been attached to the term 'standard' and tracing the usage through to the present day where it has become a touchstone of Government education policy and a term that is used, often loosely, in a great deal of public debate. He emphasizes that there is a crucial distinction between the notion of a standard as a yardstick for judging performance and a standard in the sense of the average level of attainment as measured by that yardstick. Public pronouncements often confuse these two senses.

Aldrich traces broad historical changes in levels of attainment with respect to literacy for which some kinds of generally accepted norms or yardsticks are available. These allow large changes, such as those involving the numbers of people engaged in reading, to be roughly measured and understood. Like other contributors to the symposium he also stresses the fact that there are severe definitional problems and that agreement about small or subtle changes in attainment are very difficult, if not impossible, to determine. This is evident during the second half of the twentieth century where there is much debate but little general agreement about changes in levels of literacy, and importantly, about possible reasons for any such changes.

In the second section of his paper Aldrich discusses the latter part of the 19th century in England when the 'payments by results' system was in place. He charts the introduction of a rigid student assessment system and how opposition to it grew. Many of the debates at that time prefigure contemporary debates. These debates included issues about comparing schools with very different pupil intakes, about how *minimum* achievement targets turned into *optimal* targets for achievement, about how the most and least able were neglected in pursuit of high 'pass rates', and how creativity was discouraged. In addition there was concern that the system was conducive to a 'commercialisation' of education which was harmful. Eventually the system collapsed, although some of its assumptions about 'standards' persisted. In his conclusions Aldrich suggests that the imposition of 'quick fixes' to change 'standards' is not the way truly to raise standards and that the evidence from history supports this view.

In her discussion of Aldrich, Sutherland distinguishes between a high standard which only a few will reach and a minimum standard, and traces how these separate uses of the term developed historically for different purposes. In the introduction of examinations into the Universities and the Civil Service, standards were viewed as a fixed reference point associated with high achievement. By contrast, in the implementation of the 1862 revised code, standards were seen as defining minimum achievements. Sutherland notes how opponents of the revised code, notably Matthew Arnold, associated the imposition of crude standards with a market consumer model of education. Sutherland suggests that analysis of previous debates can often raise useful questions to ask about contemporary issues.

Prais, like Sutherland, emphasises the importance of whether a standard is meant to cater for high or low achievers and discusses how any choice is related to teaching and learning. He also makes the point that a concentration on raising *average* achievements often tends to ignore associated changes in the *spread* of achievement. He suggests that curriculum and teaching changes may have a differential effect on low and high achieving pupils.

The final discussant of Aldrich's paper, Heath, looks at evidence from the General Household Survey in order to study changes in formal qualifications during the 20th century. He shows that improvements as measured by public examination results first occurred at the lowest levels of attainment and this reinforces the point made by Aldrich and Sutherland that even with the end of 'payments by results' the 19th century concern with achieving minimum standards persisted into the 20th century. In using changes in public examination grade distributions Heath acknowledges Cresswell's point that such grades do not represent absolute fixed standards and that any inferences have to rely on judgement. He goes further and argues that we should not expect a certification examination, which over time caters for different groups, to maintain the same underlying standards. He argues, nevertheless, that using the available evidence, real changes in attainment have taken place.

In the third section Cresswell argues strongly that examination standards cannot have the same level of objectivity and hence comparability as measurements in other sciences. They rely upon judgements of examiners and, while great care is taken in making those judgements, they are ultimately subjective. Examination 'standards' are accepted because examiners are trusted to make such judgements. Cresswell discusses the ways in which examiners go about their tasks and shows how all of their procedures, including the statistically based ones, ultimately rely upon subjective, albeit informed, judgement.

He argues that we should cease attempting to use examination results as a way of monitoring standards, but does suggest that a study of the way such things as examination formats and marking schemes have changed over time can provide interesting insights into how general perceptions of 'standards' may have changed.

In his discussion of Cresswell's paper, Gray suggests that a study of examiners themselves would be of interest. How are they selected; how do they maintain their professional status and how do they go about securing consensus? He suggests that examiners may need to take on board more external evidence in their quest for comparability. Such evidence may involve observations about changing student compositions, and also curriculum and assessment policies which may be politically influenced. Paterson emphasises the social construction and use of assessment judgements. He illustrates this with reference to social norms concerned with 'impartiality' and applies it to criterion referencing procedures. He characterises an exam system as a social institution continually seeking ways to allocate candidates to social roles, and illustrates his views by reference to differences between the Scottish and English exam systems. He points strongly to a need to carry out more research into the social relevance of examinations. Halsey takes a broad view of the role of examinations in modern society pointing out that some form of examination seems to be required wherever a level of competence is needed for a job. He raises questions about focussing on examinations as meritocratic selection devices.

In the final section, Bartholomew's paper explores the requirements for satisfactory measurement, starting from the proposition that there must be a fundamental requirement that agreement is reached about the way in which such standards are to be measured. He points out that there is no natural unit of measurement available and one has to be constructed. His starting point is that the quantities people are interested in, such as reading achievement, are not directly observable, and that the standard approach is therefore to use things which are observable, such as responses to specific questions, as *indicators* of the underlying attribute. The measurement process then consists in combining these indicators in suitable ways to provide an *estimate* of the quantity of interest.

Bartholomew points out that the choice of indicators is important and potentially contentious, but his concern is rather with how the responses to such indicators are combined into a measurement scale. He approaches this by envisaging a statistical *model* whose role is to relate the observed responses to the assumed underlying attribute(s) and hence to use the responses to provide estimates, for individuals and groups, of that attribute. He points out the advantages of such an approach, in that it allows various assumptions to be tested and provides a set of tools for further exploring relationships between the attributes of interest and other variables. Most important of all, it allows individuals to be distinguished by their positions along a scale, reflecting the assumption that there are indeed real differences among individuals in the attribute of interest. Any statistical model also allows us the possibility of estimating the precision with which individual or group scale values can be determined—the 'reliability' of the measuring instrument.

The broad class of models Bartholomew discusses are known as 'latent trait' or 'item response' models and he discusses how these can be formulated, how to explore their dimensionality (the number of underlying attributes) and the limitations associated with this kind of modelling. He explains very clearly how any particular statistical model can be judged by comparing its predictions against the responses actually obtained from a large random sample of respondents taking a particular test. He shows, however, that things are not always simple; often data do not allow us to distinguish between two very different models and a wide variety of assumptions may all be perfectly compatible with what is observed. He points out, however, that even though alternative explanations are possible, each may provide useful insights into individual attributes and how they interrelate. In particular he argues that some of the criticisms of mental testing have failed to understand this issue.

Finally Bartholomew considers whether a modelling perspective has something useful to contribute to debates about changing standards and presents a simple model to illustrate the real difficulties associated with making definitive statements about changes over time because we cannot separate out all the factors which are involved. He argues that the advantage of a modelling approach is that it makes clear just where the difficulties arise and hence why we can or cannot make the inferences we wish.

In his discussion of Bartholomew's paper, Goldstein looks at different possible ways of conceptualising standards and what a particular kind of definition implies for the possibility of studying differences across populations and across time. He describes two possible types; a 'constructionist' and a 'Platonic' standard. A constructionist standard is simply defined by the score on a well-specified measuring instrument. Such a score may be derived, for example, from a statistical model such as described by Bartholomew or by simply counting correct responses. What is required is agreement about how to construct and assess questions or items and how to sample individuals, and Goldstein points out some of the problems associated with such a procedure, and suggests that it is generally unattractive.

The Platonic standard is associated with attempts to conceptualise an underlying, but unobservable, attribute, which is *approximated* by a real measuring instrument; Bartholomew's discussion of constructing indicators relevant to such an attribute would be one way of operationalising this. Goldstein emphasises that what is always required is a *judgement* about how well any real instrument does in fact approximate the attribute and points out that there will generally be no agreement on this, even though some consensus may have to be reached, as in the case of public examinations. Thus, considerations of whether tests become dated over time, or whether an exam in one year measures essentially the same attributes as one in a previous year, are essentially matters for human judgement and disagreement. This leads on to a discussion of the basic weakness of Platonic standards, namely that there is no objective way of knowing whether, over time or across populations, the approximations involved are comparable or very different. He therefore echoes many of the conclusions reached by Cresswell on the subjective nature of attempts to maintain standards.

The other discussant, Plewis, reviews some of the purposes to which educational test scores can be put. He reinforces the point made by Bartholomew about the nature of the assumptions that have to be made when making comparisons over time and makes a case for studying 'second-order' changes; he argues that a study of how *inequalities* change over time may be the key matter of concern. He makes a plea for more research into the characteristics of the current National Curriculum tests on the grounds that the issues discussed in the symposium should be much better understood by those responsible for introducing and using this assessment system.

Two abiding themes seem to emerge from this set of contributions to the debate on standards in education. The first is that the very notion of a 'standard' has to be viewed in its historical and social context. Different countries have widely varying views of what constitutes a 'standard' and how necessary such a concept is for the adequate functioning of its educational system. The theme of 'trust' between educators and the public is a recurring topic here.

The second theme to emerge strongly is that it is difficult, if not impossible, to arrive at an 'objective' definition of educational standards. Despite claims to the contrary, ultimately the final appeal is to human judgement and no amount of technical sophistication can alter this. The notion of absolute standards may be attractive for many purposes, and it may also be necessary often to act *as if* comparability over time and space really did exist. Nevertheless, it is also important to recognise the inherent limitations associated with attempts to ascribe standards. Policies based upon comparisons of examinations, tests or other devices should therefore be seen for what they really are, human judgements which, however conscientiously pursued, are ultimately subjective and influenced by culture, personality and general perceptions of the external world.

A Comparative Perspective on Educational Standards

ALISON WOLF

Introduction

OVER THE LAST TWO CENTURIES, the world's education systems have developed along paths which combine major, over-arching similarities with substantial and enduring differences in philosophy and organisation. This applies to the operation of 'educational standards' as much as it does to other aspects of education. Countries all share the need to both select and certify; they chase the grail of economic growth-through-education; and they treat international surveys as a sort of mini-Olympics involving national pride and the urge to beat traditional enemies. Nonetheless, there remain profound differences between countries in how educational standards operate; and these both derive from and help sustain differences in the institutions and the values of the societies concerned.

Before turning to standards themselves, let me give some more general examples of how historical trends subsume enduring differences in countries' education systems.. Across the world, inclusive, publicly funded systems of primary and secondary education are now the norm. However, there are major differences in how far they were created by public authorities from scratch, or involved the nationalisation and integration of pre-existing voluntary provision. There are differences in the degree of autonomy that component groupings (e.g. religious schools) and individual institutions enjoy. And there are also major differences in the scale and nature of independent institutions, surviving alongside publicly funded provision.

A second example of a general trend involves the way in which

Proceedings of the British Academy, **102**, 9–37. © The British Academy 2000.

the dominant nineteenth century pattern of education, with a tiny
lycée/gymnasium/grammar school sector, teaching classics and maths,
and a unified elementary school leading into the labour market at
age 13 or 14 has been replaced, throughout the developed world, by
universal secondary schooling. Even England is now following the new
norm of full-time participation well beyond the statutory leaving age.
Yet here too major and enduring differences remain; in the extent to
which secondary provision is unified or selective, in the relative importance of work-based apprenticeship routes, in levels of centralised
curriculum control, and in the nature and impact of formal qualifications at this level. In a recent examination of trends within the EU,
colleagues and I found no evidence that secondary level education
systems were converging in anything other than size and inclusiveness
(Green, Leney and Wolf 1997; Green, Wolf and Leney 1999).

A similar picture applies when we look at qualifications and
examinations, and so enter the domain of 'standards'. Throughout
the world—and not just the developed world this time—formal
assessments and qualifications are increasing in number and importance (Dore 1996, Little and Wolf 1996, Little 1996). There are increasing government anxieties over education, because of its supposedly
critical contribution to economic growth and competitiveness, and
increasing individual (especially parental) anxieties, because of the
growing importance of formal qualifications in determining life-
chances. The management and delivery of qualifications is itself a size-
able industry.

The International Association for Educational Assessment, for
example, brings together school examination and assessment bodies
from over 50 countries: and participants find immediate common
ground because of the very limited number of ways in which this
business is organised. For the majority of the world's population
(including the citizens of China and India), secondary education is
dominated by formal educational qualifications that involve examinations set by publicly constituted or recognised examination boards,
operating with a structure of national curricula, subject committees,
common papers written under 'exam conditions' on common dates, and
paid anonymous examiners (hired largely from the teaching force). For
most others (and most notably citizens of the United States), the key
experience is of sitting standardised tests in largely multiple-choice
format, which are created and (machine) marked under conditions of
tight security by the permanent staff of testing agencies, relate to

general skills and traits rather than specific syllabi, and yield percentile scores related to national norms.

It would seem, therefore, that we have a bipolar global consensus on how to assess student achievement (or attainment of 'standards') for public reporting purposes. To this we have recently seen added a more ambitious effort, that of 'global' assessment. Here, it would seem, we really do have a common approach to the measurement and comparison of standards, as countries administer the same tests to all their students. By far the biggest player here is the IEA—the International Association for the Study of Educational Achievement. (See especially Goldstein 1995, Goldstein 1996.) The first IEA study in 1964 was a maths survey involving 12 countries and one age group (13 year olds): while for the recently completed TIMSS survey (Third International Maths and Science Study), three age groups were covered and between 40 and 50 countries participated in any given part. Many others were involved in early stages but were unable to provide the full samples required for formal reporting by the IEA. Moreover, such studies are multiplying. The IAEP (International Assessment of Educational Progress) treads similar ground to the IEA; IALS—the International Adult Literacy Survey—concerns itself with the 16–65 year old population; and the OECD is now preparing another in-depth survey of secondary students' achievement (the PISA study) involving the richer developed countries who make up its membership.

When a country participates in one of these studies, it is effectively signing up to a number of propositions: that there is a construct— mathematics achievement, literacy, or whatever—which has the same meaning for all the countries involved; that this can be measured in an equally valid way in all cases; and that the measurements can be reported in the form of a scale on which participants can be not merely ranked (higher/lower) but ascribed a mark or score which designates distance. That is, the implication is that in some meaningful way the difference between a score of (say) 45 and 55 is the 'same' as between one of 53 and 63. All of these are in fact highly questionable propositions (see especially Goldstein 1996b, McLean 1996). However, the relevant point here is that the growing number of countries participating in such studies would seem to imply a corresponding level of consensus on the nature of educational standards.

It is the argument of this paper that there is, in fact, far less of a clear consensus than the spread of international surveys, and the limited range of assessment and examining approaches, would imply.

It is not just a case of different conceptions of standards being associated with the three main approaches to 'public' assessment which have
been described—the syllabus-related exam board, the free-standing
standardised test, and the international achievement survey. Once one
examines individual countries in detail, great variability becomes
apparent even among countries which use the same basic approach.
These differences, in turn, relate to profound differences in basic values,
beliefs and objectives. The following pages demonstrate this by examining a number of exemplar countries: China, the United States, Sweden,
Germany and France.

China

As most readers will know, the first system of public examinations
which we would recognise clearly as such was developed by Imperial
China in order to select entrants to the bureaucracy of mandarins
which ran the country. Use of examinations for selecting public
servants began in the Sui dynasty (606) and continued until 1905.
The examinations were open to all; were set in relation to a fixed
syllabus; and taken under strict 'exam conditions'—uniform for all
candidates, with questions prepared secretly, and marked confidentially
by experienced examiners.

China remains a culture in which public examinations remain
critical to individual success, and are respected and trusted by the
population. It is also a culture in which one particular examination
dominates, though it is now the Entrance Examination to Higher
Education rather than the examination for entry to the Imperial civil
service. Though abolished temporarily during the Cultural Revolution,
the EEHE has otherwise, since 1952, been by far the most important
examination in P.R. China; and the general view, shared even by
academics with a critical perspective on assessment, is that 'It is universally acknowledged in China that the EEHE is beneficial to the
efficiency and quality of selection and plays an important role in
promoting the quality of secondary education.' (Wang Gang 1995: 3).

The EEHE is set by the National Education Examination Authority
in Beijing; an organisation with a network of subject committees and
officers which would be immediately recognisable to anyone from a UK
exam board. It is sat at the same time throughout the country; and
marked by university and secondary school teachers who work together,
using set marking criteria, in a seaside resort which has been taken over

for the purpose.[1] Given a school system with enrolments of 191 million pupils, this seems extraordinary, although the pyramidal nature of Chinese education means that the numbers sitting the EEHE are 'only' 2.5 million (competing for just under a million places). Nonetheless, the view of the NEEA is that any move to wholesale decentralisation would undermine faith in the examination, and create genuine dangers of corruption and political interference in the marking (personal communication).

In the last 10 to 15 years—partly because of access to Western assessment literature and debates—issues of quality and technical procedures have been debated increasingly within China; while there has also been active discussion about the nature of the examination and its backwash effects, notably about the relative emphasis on rote learning at the expense of problem-solving and critical skills. There has also been a steady refinement of the procedures for setting papers in terms of the responsibilities of subject committees, the checking of items, the pre-definition of item types, and the clarity of mark schemes.

However, the process of setting and marking papers remains fairly detached from the type of technical procedures common to American psychometrics and, to an increasing extent, English public examinations. Trialling is underway of a procedure for standardising individual subject scores before they are added up to provide the single, total score actually used for university admission. (At present, simple raw scores are used, even though different subjects tend to have markedly different means and standard deviations. See Little, Wang and Wolf, 1995.) However, there are no formal procedures in place to examine or secure standards from year to year. Since the composition of subject committees changes frequently, the main sources of stability are the well-established expectations of the student and teacher population, enshrined in the limited number of approved textbooks, and maintained through the publication of exam papers, and the expertise of committee chairmen and NEEA staff.

Ensuring strict comparability of standards from year to year has never been an issue in China, and the functions of the examination make it unlikely that it will become so. The EEHE is a selection exam: it exists in order to decide which students will be admitted into which universities.: its concerns are with 'differentiation and discrimination'

---

[1] There is one exception: Shanghai currently is permitted to set and administer its own version of the EEHE.

(Wang Binhua 1995: 32). According to the marks received, students may win admission into one of the 'key' universities which recruit nationally, or into a less desirable regional (provincial) university. The whole process is centrally steered, in the sense that the national ministry decides, every year, the total number of student enrolments which will be allowed from each province for both the provincial and the key universities. The score line above which students are eligible for the key universities varies among provinces, in order to ensure that some students are admitted from poorer, rural provinces, rather than simply from the Eastern seaboard; but with this proviso, the process is simply one of admitting the highest scoring candidates. A similar situation obtains in the case of secondary schools, where there is fierce competition for entry into the selective 'key' schools: and where entry is again decided totally on the basis of students' (raw) scores on locally set examinations.

There are two reasons why, in this context, year-on-year standards have not been an issue. The first is that, for the overwhelming majority of stakeholders—students, parents, politicians, university administrators—the only relevant issue is whether the examination appears to treat *a given year's entry* fairly. Given the enormous effort that is put into developing individual items, the clear expectations about question format and content which inform this process, and the tight security surrounding the whole process, this is not usually experienced as a problem: and an individual's relative ranking is then perceived to be the result of an objective decision. Because no claims are being made about substantive achievement levels, a purely selective examination of this type avoids many of the problems associated with the notion of 'standards over time'.

The other reason why these are not a major concern is that there is in fact no over-riding commitment to year-on-year stability. This is not because the Chinese do not care about 'standards': on the contrary. But it is worth emphasising, at this point, the multiple meanings attached to the word, and especially the difference between two of the dictionary definitions. One is that a standard is 'something set up and established by authority *as a rule for the measure of quantity, weight, extent, value or quality'*. However, another notes that standards may mean 'something established by authority, custom or general consent *as a model or example*' (Websters New Collegiate Dictionary: italics ours).

The Chinese commitment is less to the idea of standards as a measuring tool than to standards as an example and ideal. Their purpose is not to create a benchmark and guarantee a lack of change but rather to encourage and provide incentives for continuous improvement. If more and more students reach the old pass mark for a key school or university, this is not seen as a problem, or a *prima facie* indication that the paper-setters have got something wrong: but rather as a response by the student population, reflecting hard work and achievement, which is to be welcomed and encouraged. The pass mark can be raised, and the exams will have achieved one of their purposes in providing a model and an example to strive after. The same principle justifies the whole key school approach, whereby favoured schools receive greater resources as well as the highest-achieving students. The authorities 'give them more and better resources in order to allow them to become 'models' for ordinary schools. Then the experience of key schools can be extended to improve ordinary schools' (Wang Gang 1995: 2).[2] Compared to this (generally accepted) objective, issues of equality of access are irrelevant.

United States

In some respects, China and the United States provide a dramatic contrast. The rhetoric of the one is as inclusive and egalitarian as the other—post-Cultural Revolution—is élitist. The American ideal is the comprehensive high school, not the selective key school; and political and legal action for over four decades has been devoted—albeit with very little success—to equalising the expenditures and quality of education available to all children in the public (state) schools. As a country whose per capita income is approximately fifteen times that of China, it can also afford a vast tertiary sector, in which anyone who wants to study can find a place, and where over a third of the working age population has gained some form of tertiary qualification. At the same time, this sector is similar to China's in one extremely important respect. It is highly diverse and highly hierarchical, in terms of entry requirements, and the perceived value of qualifications received. No-one pretends that

---

[2] Although the Chinese have participated in IEA studies, they have not provided anything that could be seen as a representative sample of students allowing for full comparisons with other countries. Most of the participating students have come from favoured East Coast schools, and American critics have seen this as a sign that the Chinese are trying to 'cheat' and get better results than they should. But from the Chinese point of view, the interesting question *is* whether their best students can 'beat' the rest of the world (to which these results will provide an answer).

'standards' are the same across the sector, or believes that it would be sensible, let alone practicable, for them to be so.

As most people know, the United States is also very distinctive in the nature of its educational assessment. The majority of tests used for high stakes purposes are developed and sold by independent companies, not by government-run or government-regulated agencies. Seven companies dominate testing, and in some sectors, just one or two companies do so—notably ETS and ACT at college level. (Fremer 1989) A large and growing number of commercially produced tests are used within elementary and secondary schools as well: for example, from 1970 to 1991 ETS revenues showed a compound annual growth rate of 11 per cent (Madaus and Raczek 1996). This growth partly reflects increasing use of tests by teachers for internal purposes (diagnosis, promotion decisions, information for parents) and partly increased demands by school district administrators and politicians for testing, in order to increase the 'accountability' of schools, and, supposedly, improve performance.

In spite of the explosion of test use, American students are only very rarely in a position where results on these tests have high stakes consequences. A very large part of the marking, grading, and certification that takes place in American education is completely separate from the testing industry's activities. High school diplomas are given essentially on the basis of grades awarded by class teachers, who *may* take some notice of test results (and often do not: Firestone 1998). Although many states are now introducing state-wide tests which must be passed in order to graduate, these are minimum-competency tests, and as such, low-stakes for most candidates. For the majority, their Grade Point Average is far more important than simple acquisition of a high school diploma; what it records is the average of entirely teacher-given grades. College degrees are gained, again, on the basis of teacher-awarded grades, obtained on a course by course (module by module) basis. In all these contexts, the English observer is struck by the teacher's total autonomy, and by the absence of moderation, quality checks, or even the most minimal form of double marking.

Not surprisingly, this creates problems of interpretation for those involved in large-scale selection activities. Selectors take it as given that standards (and so the meaning of a Grade Point Average) will vary from high school to high school, college to college. This may not matter if you are a small-town employer selecting from one or two schools' graduates: equally, at national level, most people will recognise the best and most prestigious universities' names and weight their ranking and decisions accordingly. However, large-scale selection processes, such as characterise entry into undergraduate and graduate programmes in higher education, demand a simple, robust metric if they are to be practical and cost-effective. They also need to be defensible as 'objective'—especially in the United States, where legislative challenges play the regulatory role allocated elsewhere to national ministries and government agencies.

As a result, two tests—the SAT (Scholastic Aptitude Test) at college entry and the GRE (Graduate Record Examination) at graduate school entry—have become enormously important, high-stakes tests for young people seeking entry to higher education courses. Smaller, but equally high-stakes tests are important in specialised areas (e.g. entry to medical or law school); and there has been rapid growth in the subject-based Advanced Placement tests which give university credit (and also help win admission to the most selective schools, even where they will not give formal course credit against them). The SAT, GRE and related tests have been subject to consistent criticism on a number of counts, mostly from the professional assessment community, but also for their possible 'adverse impact' on particular groups of candidates. However, their importance has been increasing rather than decreasing; they have repeatedly met the key requirement, within American society, of satisfying the courts' criteria for an acceptable selection mechanism.

The development of American tests follows very well-established and enduring procedures. Although there has, in recent years, been a strong interest in breaking away from this, for example by developing 'authentic assessments', 'portfolios' and the like, these account for a tiny portion of testing and test development activity. (Koretz, Broadfoot and Wolf, 1998) The bulk remains firmly in the psychometric tradition, and produces tests which are commonly referred to as 'standardised' and/or 'objective'.

To describe a test as standardised is not really to do any more than indicate that scores have been transformed to fit a common metric—thus, the whole Japanese population is by now entirely used to expressing and discussing pupils' exam results in terms of 'Standard Deviation scores' (proportion of a SD above or below the mean). However, the term has also become associated, inside and outside the USA, with a particular approach and format: with the use of machine-markable multiple choice items, not tied to a particular school district or state syllabus, selected from a larger group of trialled questions on the basis of the way the various items 'behaved' during trialling. US tests are generally normed on a large sample of the target population, meaning that results can be reported in terms of a national percentile rank or other norm-referenced scale, so that one knows how a given candidate scored relative to the national population. The SATs in particular, however, are also reported in the form of actual scores.

There is an enormous literature on the underlying assumptions or 'theories' of psychometric test construction (which also dominate the development of international surveys, including the IEA surveys and those of the OECD). I will make no attempt o summarise them here (though interested readers are referred to Wood 1991, Hambleton and Zaal 1991, Goldstein and Wood 1989, Goldstein 1996) However, the testing industry in its present form has two consequences which are highly relevant to the current topic. First, judgements about content and item format, and therefore about what a given level of success actually involves or means, are completely buried from sight. They take place at a quite early stage of a test's development, with far less scrutiny than is later given to the actual selection of test items, and with no public visibility or involvement at all. Secondly, partly because of the apparent statistical complexity and difficulty of test construction, there is a high level of public confidence in the objectivity of the tests, and in the presence of procedures which ensure comparability from one year and one test form to another.

The main preoccupation of the testing industry is not with ensuring that tests and items are equally difficult in some absolute sense, or sample exactly the same content or skills, but on whether alternative forms would produce the same *rank ordering* of individuals. If the main concern of the test industry was with some sort of absolute standard that students were supposed to achieve (as seems to be the case with the current governmental conception of National Curriculum levels); or with the effects of test items on the school curriculum, this might be a problem. But in the US context it is not. Over any short period of time, comparability and substantive standards are not actually very important, since the function of these high-stakes tests *is* so over-whelmingly one of ranking and selection.

It follows that, while 'standards' certainly are an issue in American politics, comparability of test standards, year on year, has not been. However, what the US shares with the UK is a culture of political suspicion of educators, a conviction that the country's education system is uniquely poor because teachers are no good, and a faith that political reform (including use of supposedly 'objective' tests for accountability purposes) can help. This conviction has been fuelled by a number of specific events. One was the decline in SAT scores during the 1970s, which occurred fast enough to suggest a real decline in achievement (and fast enough not to be obscured by the regular re-norming of the test), and was never fully explained.[3] Another has been the recent performance of American children on international mathematics surveys (including the IEA's maths and science surveys, SIMSS and TIMSS).

In response to the TIMSS results, the US federal government is encouraging states and districts to use the TIMSS tests with their eighth grade students as part of a 'Benchmarking' exercise. The idea is to use the tests as a way of developing fixed benchmarks or 'performance standards': i.e. standards in the sense of a 'rule for the measure of quantity . . .' Such a notion has not been central to the functioning of American education in the past, and, unless there are enormous changes in selection procedures for higher education and the professions, it seems unlikely ever to have the force the Feds desire. A commitment to local and state control of education predisposes politicians and educators alike to reject any central yardstick. The size and the complexity of the sorting process between high school and college, and between undergraduate and graduate programmes are also crucial. They militate against any uniform and simple set of 'standards' becoming a basis for certification or selection.

Sweden

To move from the US to Sweden is to turn from a country whose education appears test-dominated to one where testing seems invisible. Sweden does not fit either of the dominant models outlined above: it has no examination boards or public examinations, and no widely-used standardised tests. It does, however, participate in the international tests—IEA and IALS for example—and takes them very seriously.

For a small country, Sweden has also received an unusual amount of attention over the last 50 years, especially from economists and political scientists. Its combination of extremely wide-ranging welfare state provision and high tax rates with a highly successful economy, encompassing a number of world-class companies (Ericsson, ABB, Volvo etc),

---

[3] In spite of extensive and impassioned debate, and copious research, it remains unclear whether there was any major downturn in achievement, or why. See e.g. Stedman (1998).

has led many commentators to seek both insights and recommendations for their home countries. In recent years the 'Swedish model' has
been less generally successful, and subject to criticism and modification
at home: but the country's social policies and ethos remain highly
distinctive.

Many educationalists, if asked what they knew about Swedish education, would reply that the country has no external public examinations. This is, in fact, only half true. What is true is that, like the United
States, Sweden has no formal final examinations on which leaving
certificates or university entrance are based. However, there *are*
national tests, used at key points during secondary education; and their
nature, purpose and history indicate a great deal about the Swedish
approach to 'standards'.

As in many other countries, Swedish education and assessment are
currently in the process of reform. The changes will affect the nature of
the national tests, but at the moment they are still at a trial stage (and
encountering serious implementation problems). The final shape of the
reforms is not yet clear, and the discussion here largely describes the
'old' system; but the basic purpose of the tests, and the role of teacher
assessment will in any case remain unchanged.[4]

There are two major points of assessment which affect a Swedish
pupil's future path. The first is at the end of ninth grade, when all
subjects that the pupil is studying are assessed by the relevant subject
teacher, and given a mark: historically from 1 (lowest) to 5 (highest)
although under current reforms this is being changed to a four-level
scale. The number of subjects could total as many as 15 or 16 subjects,
and all subjects count towards a student's final assessment and set of
marks, which is simply an unweighted average. The second major
assessment is at the end of twelfth grade when the same procedures
apply.

The assessment at the end of compulsory school (9th grade) determines admission to different courses within the upper secondary
school, or (for a decreasing number) affects labour market entry; and
the assessment at the end of 12th grade determines admission to
university, or, again, is important in making job applications. In 12th
as in 9th grade, up to 15 subjects are taken and all count equally. (Thus
the mark for a one semester course in child care could in theory count

---

[4] A major purpose of the reforms is to make tests and teacher assessments alike more
criterion-based and less norm-referenced.

for as much as the maths mark or Swedish grade. In practice, everyone gets a more or less equivalent mark for this course.) Almost all Swedish students now proceed directly to upper secondary school after 9th grade. Here, recent reforms have made the vocational and academic options in upper secondary school the same length (three years) and much more similar than in the past. However there is still a clear distinction between them, related (among other things) both to the school marks required for admission, and to the university programmes whose prerequisites they meet.

Admission to both upper secondary programmes and university is made on the basis of the marks awarded by teachers (using a 1 to 5 scale) at the end of the 9th and 12th grades respectively. However, a number of national tests exist which are designed to ensure comparability of standards across the country. Under current arrangements the first national test of students take place in the first semester of grade 8. This covers English, and is followed by tests of Maths and Swedish in grade 9 (the end of compulsory school).

The tests are written by university-based groups in education faculties, who draw on the national curriculum and their own experience to prepare the items. They are taken by all students, and are used by teachers to standardise their own marks. However they do *not* override them. They work as follows.

All students take the tests, and a large sample of scripts is marked and analysed centrally, providing a mark distribution which can be divided up into 5 bands equivalent to the grading 1 through 5. This corresponds to the 5 level scale used for the official assessment by the teachers. (The use of a five-level scale dates back to 1962. Before that, 7 levels were used.)

The bands or scale followed the normal distribution quite strictly in the early days, so that the percentage of pupils falling into each band nationally was as follows (Kilpatrick and Johansson 1994):

Band	1	2	3	4	5
Percentage of Pupils	7	24	38	24	7

More recently the norming system for grade 9 was changed. Guidance states that the mean should be 3 for the country as a whole, and that there should be more 4s and 2s in a *class* (sic) than 5s and 1s respectively (Skolöverstyrelsen 1980: quoted in Kilpatrick and Johansson. See also Wolf and Steedman 1998) Nationally, about 40 per cent do indeed get a 3; 30 per cent get a 1 or a 2, and 30 per cent a 4 or a 5. No information is compiled on the breakdown between 1s and 2s and 4s and 5s. However, given that there was a lot of unhappiness about giving low grades—particularly 1s—and that this affected the move away from the standard grade distributions of the 1960s, it seems likely that there are fewer 1s than a normal distribution would imply.

The purpose of the national tests is, as noted above, to help the teachers standardise their own marking. The teachers mark the tests themselves, and so know exactly what raw scores each child has obtained; but *there is no direct link between an individual child's test and end-of-year score.* Instead, the information from the national analysis tells a school what proportion of its students should, at the end of the day, fall into a given category. So if, for example, the marks which students get on the test indicate that 40 per cent fall in band 3, then the teachers and school must stick to that in their final grades. Their distribution of grades for, say, Maths or Swedish—the standardised subjects—should provide for 40 per cent receiving grade 3s, even though the individual students getting a 3 at year end may not be the same as the ones who got marks in the grade 3 band on the test itself.

In the past, teachers were told which raw test scores corresponded to which grades for all 5 grades, and so could align their mark distribution exactly with that suggested by the national test results. More recently, in line with the more permissive (some would say ambiguous) marking guidance, they have been told only which set of scores covered the middle grade (grade 3). No guidance is given on where the mark cut-off between grade 2 and grade 1 lies, or the one between 4 and 5. If 30 per cent of the school's cohort scored higher than the grade 3 band of marks, it is up to the school where it puts the higher boundary, and how it allocates that 30 per cent to the two grades.[5]

This process is quite straightforward for teachers in subjects with a national test. In others they have to use other methods—e.g. comparing science results with those in maths, on the assumption there should be some relationship. There is group discussion of the grades in many schools; and the head, who has ultimate responsibility, will ask for grades to be justified.

The remarkable aspect of the Swedish approach is the way it lodges final judgements with teachers, as those best placed to know a pupil's performance; but uses testing not to replace but to improve

---

[5] In fact in Maths the way results are reported makes it possible for teachers to calculate the marks for each band quite easily, should they wish.

that judgement. For the British outsider, however, it is natural to ask how this system can actually deliver genuinely consistent judgements, especially in the subjects not covered by the tests; and how it can survive given the extremely high stakes nature of some of the judgements made. At entry to upper secondary school, where 9th grade marks determine which upper secondary programme a student can enter, there is considerable room for flexibility, discussion with the students and parents, and, indeed, school autonomy in deciding whether or not to admit a student to the desired course. At university level, however, no such flexibility is found. Entry to Swedish university courses is strictly on the basis of marks: candidates are ranked, and places are allocated in strict descending order. If one place is left, and there is a difference of 0.1 in the average marks of the two remaining applicants, the place goes automatically to the higher scoring candidate.[6] To make allowances for the fact that a student comes from a poor background, or a small rural school, or has faced family problems in the preceding year—as Oxford or Cambridge selectors do routinely— is completely outside the powers of a comparably important faculty at the Universities of Stockholm, Uppsala or Gothenburg.

In the Chinese case, we have seen how the main objective of the university entrance procedure is to secure and improve the level achieved by the highest achievers, and to identify them in a 'fair' way, rather than to attempt to identify underlying aptitudes, let alone use the selection system to redress (even partially) underlying inequalities of opportunity. In the Swedish case, however, this interpretation seems implausible, and is, indeed, completely at odds with the egalitarian and inclusive philosophy which, still, marks out Swedish culture and politics. How is it then, that the education system and society at large should evince such a stable and long-standing lack of concern over whether standards are equal between schools, or subjects, or years?

The answer is, I would suggest, to be found in a different aspect of that same culture, which, in this case, takes precedence: a belief in consensus and a corresponding tendency to respect and indeed build up the power of professionals and professional groups, rather than seeing them as essentially a conspiracy against the public interest. This is a theme to which I shall be returning in some detail at the

---

[6] There is, in fact, since 1991 a fail-safe mechanism in the form of an aptitude test which students can take; and which may be used partially to substitute for school marks.

end of this paper; but in the Swedish context, it means that education policy is conducted with rather than against the teachers, who value and defend their traditional role as student assessors, and who are seen as the best-placed to deliver those judgements. None of the Swedish education reforms of the last fifteen years, which include efforts by the conservative government of the early 1990s to encourage independent schools, competition between universities, and closer links to industry, have involved any significant questioning of the teachers' position as assessors and so promulgators of 'standards'. Standards are not an issue because the competence of their guardians is not an issue either; and because standards are also seen as a dimension of people's expertise, not as embodied in external mechanisms and instruments.

France and Germany

The final ports of call on this rather odd Cooks tour are our two largest European neighbours, France and Germany. Very different from each other in all but two crucial respects, their examination systems bear a close resemblance to, respectively, those of China and Sweden; and will therefore be described relatively briefly.

France possesses a large number of recognised national diplomas awarded outside the universities, all of them assessed entirely or in large part through public examination: of which the baccalauréat is the largest and most important. The papers for these examinations are set centrally, by the Ministry of Education, using questions selected from among large numbers contributed by the regional offices—the *Rectorats*, one per *Académie*—which have, among their duties, the actual conduct of the examinations. This process is taken extremely seriously, in the sense that the papers—taken at exactly the same time, under classic 'exam conditions', by all candidates—are published and distributed under conditions of extreme confidentiality; marked under the supervision of the *Rectorat* officials; and the results ratified by an officially constituted *jury*.

This process is regarded as central to establishing and maintaining an objective and fair system, in which candidates succeed on their merits. While French commentators, most notably Pierre Bourdieu (1989), have subjected this belief in the system's fairness to sustained criticism, it remains strong. The continuing commitment of the French élite to centralised control over education is itself linked to a conviction that only in this way can one sustain a system of national diplomas: that is, diplomas which are recognised as objective, consistent, and equally valuable whoever the holder, and wherever and whenever they were obtained. However, by English or American standards, the actual process of examination setting and marking is remarkable for its almost total neglect of 'technical' procedures such as item scrutiny, comparability exercises to check inter-*Académie* marking consistency, archiving of scripts etc. There is fairly little checking of teacher-markers' scoring, and no national appeal procedure. Instead, it is assumed that, on substantive issues relating to standards, the professional expertise of those setting the questions will ensure acceptable levels of consistency and curriculum fidelity.

The German system is even more free of technical procedures but in other ways a total contrast to the French. The German secondary school system is (broadly) tripartite, with vocational, technical and academic schools (*Hauptschulen, Realschulen, Gymnasien*), each of which leads to a school leaving certificate which is gained on the basis of examinations. Only the certificate from a *Gymnasium*—the *Abitur*—allows entry to university, although the *Realschulen* certificates allow holders to enter polytechnic (*Fachhochschulen*) courses.

In every case, the school leaving certificate is awarded on the basis of internal examinations and marks, awarded by students' own teachers. The expected standards are defined in written documents produced by the standing conference of state ministers (since education, in Germany, is a state not a federal responsibility.) In some states (*Länder*) the topics for the written examinations are set at state level; elsewhere, schools submit topics which must be approved (to establish common expectations across schools) but are their own responsibility. Marking is entirely internal, with the school principal having the responsibility to maintain and monitor standards.

I noted above that these apparently quite disparate systems of France and Germany do have two important characteristics in common. The first of these is that, unlike England, both have experienced an enormous increase in numbers of candidates and diploma-holders without also experiencing serious loss of confidence in the system. In France, a government commitment to have 80 per cent of the age cohort completing baccalauréat programmes (though not necessarily passing the exams) has almost been realised, involving more than a doubling of participation rates since 1985. In Germany, the percentage obtaining the *Abitur* has risen from 5 per cent in 1960 to 25 per cent in the early 80s to over a third today.

There are, of course, some concerns about resulting achievement levels. In France, a good part of the increase in baccalauréat student numbers is found in programmes leading to the vocational bac (*baccal auréat professionel*) rather than the traditional academic courses. These vocational baccalauréats are seen as definitely of lower status, and few holders go on to university. But a very large part of the increase has been in 'general' bac. numbers, and here, especially when compared to English worries over A level standards, confidence has by and large been maintained. A similar situation obtains in Germany. There are worries about comparability of standards, but these centre around the conviction of the Bavarians that all the other *Länder* are operating with lower standards than they are. Moreover, this is not a serious issue; threats by the Bavarians to refuse to allow *Abitur*-holders from other states automatic entrance to Bavarian universities have come to nothing, and the German population generally shows a continuing confidence in both the quality of its schools and the reliability and worth of their certificates.

The other major similarity between the two countries is their reliance on professional judgement and expertise, and corresponding absence of any widespread culture of assessment expertise, concerns with statistically based quality control, and the like. I will not speculate on how far this absence is a cause rather than a result of politicians' willingness to accept professional control, and to leave the general conduct of educational policy—whether reformist as in France, or highly stable as in Germany—to their officials and teachers. However, it is worth noting how differently educational interest and identity group boundaries run, as compared to England (but perhaps not Scotland.)

Far from seeing the *Académies* as rivals for power, as English ministries and quangos see the local authorities and exam boards, the French operate a centralised system in which the senior officials at the Ministry of Education form part of the same group as those who run the regions and the examinations. In Germany, teachers are civil servants, and enjoy both the respect and the protection this implies. Challenging, or allowing challenges to, their assessment authority would call into question the position of public servants throughout the educational (and other) spheres. In the absence of any general concern over standards, it is thus not surprising that neither country's politicians has shown the slightest inclination to open up the assessment process to public scrutiny, by, for example, instituting rights of appeal, oversight committees or sponsoring large-scale research studies on comparability-related issues.[7]

However, there is also a link between levels of public concern over standards and the role those standards play in determining students' lives. While both France and Germany use school-leaving examinations to determine university entrance, their higher education systems are very different from the highly hierarchical and internally differentiated Anglo-Saxon (or Chinese) ones. Leaving aside the French *Grandes Écoles*, which operate their own formal entrance examinations, both countries essentially allow university entrance to all holders of the relevant diploma. Thus, in Germany, an *Abitur* holder can study any degree in any university in the country. (The only major exception is medicine, where the *numerus clausus* system holds, and a tiny fraction of a mark can make the difference between success and failure to win a place. Significantly, here there are alternative routes and fail-safe procedures which allocate about 20 per cent of the places differently.) In France, there are tighter requirements for prerequisite subjects: but again, anyone with a 'general' (academic) bac. can be sure of a place. Most students study locally: and the important thing is that one passes one's bac, rather than how well one passes. In consequence, while the certificates are high stakes, it is only one boundary (pass/fail) that really matters. It is not that important to most students' chances whether they got precisely the right mark. In other words, compared to England, *only a small proportion of students have a strong, personal interest in the precision of the marking*, and they are not the most successful or visible ones. This, too, tends to reduce the pressure on the system to deliver apparent comparability within and across years; and also reduces the extent to which standards become a public and political issue.

Conclusions

The limited number of ways in which countries organise high-stakes examinations and diplomas suggests an equally common approach to maintaining 'standards'. The previous discussion will hopefully have indicated that this is not the case. In fact, the way countries operate,

---

[7] The recent refusal of the French to allow publication of the French results from the International Adult Literacy Survey may reflect not merely a refusal to countenance, let alone admit, that French adults could be performing poorly, but also concerns over the public impact of any such findings.

and the degree to which aspects of 'standards' become contentious, can only really be understood in terms of far wider aspects of political and organisational cultures. It is not because they operate with such different assessment systems that the United States and Germany are hugely different in the extent of political concern over educational standards. Rather, in each case, the assessment and certification systems must be understood in terms of higher education structures, the role of legislation and litigation, and deeply embedded attitudes towards the position of public servants (including teachers), and the efficacy and respect due to regulations.

A number of other points suggest themselves. The first is that *England—and indeed the UK—is extremely unusual in its overt claim that 'standards' are being maintained from year to year in some absolute sense*, and in the primacy of criterion-related concerns over norm-referencing practices. Other countries may make the implicit assumption that 'standards' are being held constant, in the sense of some measure which yields the same quantity year or year; but they certainly do not make models of performance or notions of benchmarking the centrepiece of their item-writing, examining and moderating procedures in the way the UK examination boards have done for many decades. Conversely, other countries tend to be much more overtly focused on the process of differentiation and selection, through a more or less explicit norm-referencing approach. It is commonplace to argue that certificates such as A levels have the dual function of certification and selection, and that the latter function is dominant. However, compared to most countries, what is striking about the UK is that we tend to spend most of our effort on procedures and concerns which are more relevant to certification than to selection pure and simple.

The second point which strikes one is that transparency and public confidence are by no means positively correlated—perhaps the opposite. In countries where the assessment process is left very much to the teachers and educational professionals, there appears to be less, not more anxiety over standards. It is always difficult to know which way lines of causality run, and the increasing extent to which the examination process in the UK is overseen, dissected, and opened up to appeal is certainly in part a response to, rather than a cause of, public unease (Wolf 1995). But given the inherently imperfect and non-mechanical nature of assessment judgements, and the UK's unusually ambitious claims regarding standards over time, one may doubt that further auditing and oversight will increase confidence, and predict that it is more likely to decrease it further.

The third and final point follows on from this. Whichever country one looks at, it is clear that, ultimately, 'standards' do depend on professional judgement. From an English standpoint, we may be somewhat unimpressed by French or German neglect of comparability studies and agreement trials, or by their level of attention to checking marks and markers; or see much of the underlying 'theory' in US psychometrics as a combination of the doubtful and the true-by-definition. Nonetheless, at root, all of these countries, like our own, build their systems on the foundation of professional knowledge and professional judgement about what to ask, and how to assess the response.

This irreducible fact runs counter to a set of beliefs which are especially powerful at present in Anglo-Saxon societies but increasingly influential elsewhere as well, and which demand 'accountability', 'openness' and demonstrated 'value for money'. In a recent book called *The Audit Society: Rituals of Verification*, the LSE's Michael Power has described in detail how pervasive these ideas have become, not just in education but in the whole area of regulation within organisations as well as across sectors. Unfortunately, in almost every case, whether one is talking about the auditing of a company; new management techniques for the Health Service; the quality management approaches being introduced into higher education across Europe; or the growing use of tests by British and American politicians, it is extremely unclear just what is being measured, or what can be done with the information. Things get counted because things have been found or created which are countable: as Power puts it, 'audits work because organisations have literally been made auditable; audit demands the environment, in the form of systems, and performance measures, which make a certain type of verification possible' (1997: 91).

This movement is in part a result of a messianic belief in the power of these approaches to make things 'better': more efficient, fairer, more productive. However, they are also a result of a breakdown in trust, and especially in trust in professional groups. It is not clear to me how far this is a cumulative and more or less inevitable component of all modern societies, as I suppose some sociologists such as Habermas would argue; and how far it is associated with more specific movements and analyses, such as the distrust of all organised groups, as conspiracies against the public, which marked the Thatcher years.

Either way, an absence of trust is not really sustainable, because, while trust is always fragile, it is also completely necessary to the functioning of social life, and certainly to the operation of any system of educational certification and selection. If we cannot restore and improve public and political trust in our current 'standards' there is a risk that we will follow the American example and be forced into restoring confidence by establishing new and totally *non*-transparent 'expert systems', dominated by issues of reliability. We would, in the process, end up with an increasingly constrained form of public examination whose apparently 'objective' nature merely hides the value judgements and decisions inherent in any assessment. It would be far more desirable, in my view, to learn from other countries that effective learning and high standards do not require a supposedly 'ever-fixèd mark'; something that in education (if not in love) is in any case quite unattainable.

Discussion

Julia Whitburn

Professor Wolf has provided us with an admirably clear exposition to support her thesis that there is little international consensus regarding methods of assessment. She has also argued that the lack of consensus reflects differences in basic values, beliefs and educational objectives of the countries concerned. I do not wish to dispute her main argument but rather to offer a few comments on the value of a comparative perspective with regard to the issue of educational standards.

The significance of a comparative perspective is perhaps most immediately apparent in the context of the large international studies of achievement, notably those by the International Association for the evaluation of Educational Achievement (IEA) and the most recent Third International Mathematics and Science Study (TIMSS). Despite the well-documented difficulties of making valid trans-national comparisons, such studies are here to stay, and it is only fair to say that many of the methodological deficiencies of the First International Mathematics Study (FIMS) were addressed by the time of the third study. Lessons to be learned from these studies fall, I would suggest, into three categories. First, we see, albeit crudely, how we stand in the international league table of results. This gives our national pride, which thrives on the spirit of competition and knowing how our achievements stand in relation to those of others, a blow when we look at mathematics attainments but a boost when we quickly turn to the science results.

The second lesson, however, is perhaps of greater importance: we learn that simplistic comparisons of educational systems and results are both misleading and dangerous, and that the multi-factorial and complex nature of the educational arena is aggravated by the cultural contextualisation. In spite of this, however, as Professor Wolf has indicated, countries do 'sign up' to the proposition that there is an 'educational construct' that has a commonality of meaning and relevance for all countries involved and that this can be quantified in an adequately valid way.

The third lesson to be learned from international studies comes in our attempt to turn from looking outwards to the achievements of other countries to looking inwards to our own achievements. International studies help to ensure that the debate over performance standards is informed by our understanding of the details of educational systems and circumstances prevailing in other countries, and lead us to ask ourselves questions about the *structure* of our own educational system, which we might otherwise not have asked. This third lesson, I believe, is the one that, in any educational context, represents the real value of a comparative perspective.

Professor Wolf has, in her paper, interpreted educational standards as the measuring of achievement by pupils within a single country and she has drawn to our attention the different and contrasting approaches to assessment or output measures. The real question is 'What does this comparative dimension add to our understanding of, or debate on, measuring achievement?'

First, we become aware that if we are to judge by the amount of testing, in England there is a great concern with standards. English pupils are tested on a nation-wide basis more frequently than pupils in many other countries. Some countries have no system of national testing of all pupils at any stage, for example, in Japan, which is one of the highest achieving countries in terms of average mathematical attainment. In Switzerland another high-attaining country mathematically there is no point during the period of compulsory formal schooling at which all pupils are routinely assessed using a standardised test, although the highest attaining pupils attending *Gymnasien* may obtain the *Maturität* or school-leaving examination equivalent perhaps to that of the *Abitur* (of the better schools) in Germany. In contrast, *all* pupils in England are tested by nationally standard tests at ages 7, 11, 14 and 16, at the end of each Key Stage during compulsory schooling. In addition, a national system of Baseline Assessment of all children on entry to schooling has just been introduced. Increasingly, schools choose to administer additional School Assessment Tests (SATs) tests between KS1 and KS2, and, on leaving school, a high proportion of pupils also take 'A' level examinations or other forms of assessment at 18.

A comparative perspective makes us consider more carefully what the *purpose* of this testing is and to ask whether or not it could be achieved better in other ways. At 16 and at 18, testing may be justified on the basis of certification of individual pupils and/or selection for employment or the next stage of education (the latter reason is probably more relevant to 'A' level assessment). Testing at Key Stages 1, 2 and 3, however, is unrelated to the certification or selection of individual pupils. Indeed, results relating to the performance of individual pupils are available to parents only in the most general form in terms of *level* gained, defined very broadly.

While it must be a source of reassurance for parents to know that their child has achieved at least the so-called 'expected' level 2 at age 7, this is scarcely a reason for congratulation. In 1997, for example, the level was achieved by 84% of children. (Schools may inform parents as to whether their 7-year-old child got a Level 2c, 2b or 2a, but the amount of explanation provided varies from school to school.) In fact, analysis of SATs results tends to focus more on *results at school levels* and for *schools* to be congratulated on the improvement to their achievements. (This is also now true of GCSE and 'A' Level results, where league tables of *school* results highlight the best and worst.) We are all aware that making simplistic comparisons of school achievements can be misleading.

Indeed, these are arguably more dangerous than simplistic *transnational* comparisons since we are not able to perform the multifactorial analysis of school situations that we recognise as necessary for valid international comparisons. But why is it that in England our obsession is with comparing *school* performance? Does it reflect our mistrust of our schools and our teachers which has been fuelled by those in influential positions? Or is it more a reflection of our unwillingness to attribute individual responsibility for achievement (or failure)? In Japan, there is a widespread belief in the importance of effort rather than innate ability and *pupils* are encouraged that 'If you work hard enough and persevere, you can succeed.' In England, I would suggest, the message is that *teachers* need to work harder and persevere in order for their pupils to succeed and where pupils do not achieve well, it is poor teaching that is held to be responsible. From the view that teachers and schools are to be blamed for their pupils' poor achievements it is only a small step to the system of payment by results which operated in schools over 100 years ago, as described by Professor Aldrich. Indeed, there are already financial consequences for low-achieving schools since lower enrolment of pupils which can follow publication of their poor league table rankings then adversely affects their subsequent funding levels. Incidentally, if the purpose of national tests is to monitor school rather than pupil performance, it is possible that this could be achieved effectively and at a lower cost by using sampling rather as the APU did at an earlier time.

But that is a digression. If our tests are to be about school rather than individual achievement, this suggests that they may be moving towards a concept of 'expected standards' as outlined by Professor Aldrich. We need to be very careful, however as Sig Prais has already explained in our use of the term 'expected standards'. The statement that by 2002 '75% of 11-year-olds will be reaching the standards expected for their age in maths' implies a curious distribution of mathematics scores. What, perhaps, the government hopes to achieve by 2002 is for 75% of 11-year-olds to be achieving a specified *minimum* standard.

This brings me to the third question that benefits from a comparative perspective, namely, what can we learn in relation to the concept of minimum standards by considering other educational systems? The concept of a minimum standard for a particular grade level is not uncommon and may be found in other countries such as France, Switzerland and Germany. In each of these countries, a pupil's progress to a subsequent grade is contingent on his/her satisfactorily achieving the minimum standard. What we find, however, is that to enable all pupils to achieve the minimum standards, certain modifications or additions to educational systems develop. For example, we have the practice of *'redoublement'* in France, known as *'sitzen bleiben'* in Germany, and *'repetieren'* in Switzerland in conjunction there with the more important element of age-flexibility on entry to schooling. In Japan, the private tutorial system of *'juku'* is an essential under-pinning for the public education system in which minimum standards are expected to be attained by all pupils. Without these practices, it is difficult to imagine that the expectation of minimum standards for all pupils could continue.

If the government is indeed proposing that 75% of all 11-year-olds should achieve a *minimum* standard, we need to ask what this standard will be, how it will be decided and what the implications are for the curriculum and for the organisation of classes and of teaching. We may wish to consider how our concept of a minimum standard compares with those of other countries. For example, if we look at the content of the Maths curriculum for elementary school children in Japan, we might conclude that the content and level of the curriculum for children aged 7 are not dissimilar to those of English pupils. If 84% of pupils achieve a Level 2, are they then not performing at a comparable level to 7-year-old pupils in Japan? All research evidence points to the fact that English pupils do *not* perform at a level comparable to Japanese pupils at this age. One reason for this apparent paradox may lie with the way in which the 'standard' required to achieve a Level 2 is set. Many of us may be familiar with the content of the tests; some may *not* dispute the *level* of *difficulty* of the questions. But are we all aware, and are we content that the *level* of the expected standard (or minimum standard) is relatively low; for example, this year for children to be awarded the 'expected' Level 2, the KS1 Mathematics test required a score of only 10 out of 36 and a similar percentage score for science?

I have mentioned only a few of the questions that we might ask in relation to educational standards: a comparative perspective helps us to focus our minds on these questions that we need to be asking in order to ensure that what is being promulgated as an 'educational standard' is of value. If we are going down on the route of minimum standards then we need to be sure we understand and agree with what that is. Pupils, parents and the country deserve this.

David Reynolds

Alison Wolf's paper makes some very important points. She notes that the apparent universality of concern about standards and the increasing international participation in surveys of achievement, and indeed the whole discourse about the results of these surveys, hide large differences between countries in how 'standards' are maintained, understood and operated.

I would venture three comments. First, I think that the paper underestimates the extent to which there is not just considerable variation between societies in their systems for ensuring standards but also in their very valuation of which 'standards' are important. It is a much neglected feature of the 'tyranny of the international horse race' that the countries who have historically done well on the various academic outcomes, measured conventionally on tests of basic skills, are now most doubtful of their value. In anglophone societies, such as the United States in the case of its maths performance at 16, and England and Wales in the case of its maths performance at 9, there is considerable attention given to the surveys and a correspondingly increasingly narrow view that academic outcomes are important. Countries doing well, such as those of the Pacific Rim, are concerned with new definitions of what 'standards' matter. Instead of any national concern about academic standards, there is a concern:

- to broaden the range of children's capacities to include more higher order skills in addition to the basic skills that the system apparently transmits so effectively;
- to focus upon social outcomes that are important for the world of work, such as children's capacity to work together collaboratively in groups;
- to encourage children to be creative and produce 'new' knowledge, and to think laterally to generate the interactions between bodies of knowledge.

These concerns are now widespread across the Pacific Rim. I would expect this cross-national variation in what constitutes the 'important standards' to increase, notwithstanding the continued popularity of academically based international studies. I would expect consequently much change in assessment systems as new outcomes become standards.

Secondly, Professor Wolf's paper misses one important international characteristic of the standards debate, which is how 'standards' are increasingly being linked to specific 'policies' and not merely seen in terms of performance on outcome measures. It is one thing to propose, as some of us have done, that we should investigate the extent to which other societies have classroom characteristics which may be useful and effective if transplanted to our own society. An example of this is the interest in Pacific Rim whole class interactive teaching. However, there appears to be an international movement to look at and potentially to adopt the national *policies*.

All this may be very damaging, however, since it may be that *different* policies may be required in *different* national contexts to generate the effective classroom teachers that may be quite *similar* in different nations. In our International School Effectiveness Research Project (ISERP) study (Reynolds et al., 1998), we have found that certain teacher instructional features are effective across nine societies (as varied as Taiwan, the United Kingdom, the United States and Australia) in discriminating ineffective schools from typical schools and from effective schools. The clear demonstration of high expectations, frequent questioning, lesson structure, use of review, pupils' time on task and teachers' capacity to manage their classrooms are factors that all exist in the effective schools of different countries. However, the school level variables and the national policies that are necessary to generate these *same* characteristics are very *different*. In a country such as Taiwan, where there is a cultural acceptance of directive political leadership, a Principal may need to be directive with teachers to get these effective classroom factors in place, because they would not discover them for themselves. In a culture such as Great Britain, such direction may not be functional. At national policy level, to speculate with another example, the use of the 'meso' level of the District or the LEA to lever up standards of teaching may be more effective in cultures where there are traditions of decentralisation to federal governments than in the United Kingdom, with its strong central government.

As 'standards' become linked to 'policies' for the obvious political reason that policies are easier to explain than processes and because one can get changes in policies quicker than in outcomes, they are tending to become more similar. I suspect by contrast that a more fruitful perspective may be the maximisation of policy variation as the means to ensure the universalisation of the same effective teaching characteristics. In any event, the 'for standards read policies' movement has considerable implications.

Thirdly, I found the comments about our British near obsession with the accountability of the educational system as resulting from the breakdown of 'trust' between educational 'producers' and the wider society, most interesting. I suspect that this breakdown reflected public perception of the wide variation in school quality that exists in the United Kingdom, a variation which school effectiveness research revealed and which politicians then exploited for political gain.

I also suspect that British teachers themselves have made the breakdown of trust more serious by their own inability to trust each other in close professional relationships. Perhaps reflecting high needs for personal autonomy, British teachers have been reluctant to permit others to see them teach, a reluctance magnified in its effects by the lack of time in which such observations can take place and the lack of observation systems of proven reliability, validity and practical applicability. More recently, the arrival of various forms of market pressures involving competition between schools and associated systems of parental choice has probably made any transfer of 'good practice' between schools as rare as such transfer between individuals.

Building on Professor Wolf's important insight, I would speculate that the way to rebuild trust by the public in education professionals is to deal with the levels of between school and within school variability, which themselves may be a direct result of the lack of trust amongst professionals in education.

Educational Standards in
Historical Perspective

RICHARD ALDRICH

Introduction

THE *Oxford English Dictionary* lists some thirty usages of the word, 'standard'. Two broad categories amongst such usages are those of a military or naval ensign and an exemplar of measure or weight. The term, 'standard', first appears in English with reference to the Battle of the Standard, fought at Northallerton between the English and Scots on 22 August 1138. A contemporary chronicler, Richard of Hexham, described the standard as a mast of a ship surmounted by flags around which the English grouped, which was called a standard because 'it was there that valour took its stand to conquer or die'. In this sense the 'raising of one's standard' meant (and still may imply) setting forth to engage in battle or other stirring deeds.

The second sense, of an authorised exemplar of measure or weight, for example the standard lengths built into the wall of the observatory at Greenwich, is connected to the first inasmuch as early usages state or imply 'the king's standard'. Just as the royal standard in battle was the place around which all should rally and from which commands were issued, so the royal or official standards or measures were those which subjects should employ in business and commercial dealings. This sense of a measure to which all objects or persons should conform was extended into many spheres of life, becoming a definite degree of quality, viewed as a measure of an adequate level for a particular purpose or as a prescribed object of endeavour. In 1862, with the introduction of the Revised Code into elementary schools, the word 'standard' took on a further meaning, defined by the *Oxford English*

Proceedings of the British Academy, **102**, 39–67. © The British Academy 2000.

Dictionary as, 'Each of the recognised degrees of proficiency, as tested by examination, according to which school children are classified'. From the end of the nineteenth century, the demise of centrally-controlled annual examinations led to the gradual disappearance of this particular connotation of the word 'standard'. Today, however, standards in education are as prominent an issue as they were a century and more ago. In 1998, a School Standards and Framework Act stands on the Statute Book, a Standards and Effectiveness Unit with more than 100 members of staff has been created within the Department for Education and Employment, while the Standards Task Force is chaired by the Secretary of State, David Blunkett, himself, with Chris Woodhead, the Chief Inspector of Schools, and Tim Brighouse, Director of Education for Birmingham, as vice-chairs.

Dictionary definitions demonstrate that the terms 'standard' and 'standards' have many different meanings. These meanings have changed over time, and will continue to do so. Confusion can, and does, occur, even in official documents. For example, the third section of the White Paper, *Excellence in Schools*, published in 1997, is entitled 'Standards and accountability'. Its first sub-heading declares, 'Raising standards: our top priority', and it reports that 'in the 1996 national tests only 6 in 10 of 11 year-olds reached the standard in mathematics and English expected for their age' (DfEE 1997: 10). Here, the term, standard, is being used in the sense of an accepted level against which all should be judged. But the raising of standards referred to in the sub-heading presumably does not apply (at least not initially) to raising the expected standards which four out of ten children were already failing to reach. Rather it refers to raising the unacceptable standards or levels of achievement of those who were failing to reach the expected standard. Indeed, the White Paper states categorically that by the year 2002

> 80% of 11 year-olds will be reaching the standards expected for their age in English; and 75% of 11 year-olds will be reaching the standards expected for their age in mathematics.
>
> (DfEE 1997: 19)

It remains to be seen whether any modification of the expected standards will be needed to ensure that these percentages are achieved.

Further questions may be identified here, questions which are historical in that they relate to continuities and changes in human purposes and judgements over time. For example, if an educational standard is defined as an authorised exemplar or measure, who defines that standard? Is it intended to be the same for all pupils of the same age? Are all pupils expected to achieve it, or is its purpose to select some and to reject others—as in the case of the eleven-plus examination which governed transition from the primary stage before the introduction of comprehensive secondary schools, or in the use of GCE Advanced level grades in selection of entrants to higher education. Standards, in common with examinations, curricula and education itself, have a history which has been contested by contemporaries and historians alike. Since 1988, government policies to improve the quality of education have been based upon the concept of an expected standard of achievement for all children of a particular age. This situation may be strongly contrasted with the advice given in the Plowden Report of 1967 which 'concluded that it is not possible to describe a standard of attainment that should be reached by all or most children. Any set standard would seriously limit the bright child and be impossibly high for the dull. What could be achieved in one school might be impossible in another' (DES 1967: i, 201–2).

In further contrast, in 1971 Cox and Dyson included the following ironic 'progressive' definition of standards: 'Irrelevant academic concept designed to exclude, or penalize, students distinguished for *either* concern *or* creativity *or* both' (Cox and Dyson 1971: 215).

Today, it is argued by central government and its agencies not only that it is necessary to define national standards, but also that the levels of educational attainment of many children are lower than they should be because the expectations of many teachers, parents and pupils are too low. Teacher, pupil and parental perceptions of importance and standards, however, may conflict. For example, Schools Council Enquiry I, *Young School Leavers,* published in 1968, showed that parents of 15 year-old leavers, unlike their teachers, placed the greatest emphasis upon doing well in studies that would enable their children to get jobs. This was understandable, given that until very recent times most children in Britain left school at the earliest opportunity and proceeded directly into employment. Similarly, in October 1998, the *Times Educational Supplement* reported that 'Parents do not share ministers' high level of concern about academic achievement in schools' (Dean 1998). Expectations of standards, in common with definitions, therefore, exhibit changes, as well as continuities, over time. Levels of expectations in terms of educational achievement are the product of a long and contested history in which governmental priorities, economic and religious doctrines, employment requirements, and social factors, including those of class and gender, as well as the expectations of teachers, parents and pupils, have loomed large.

The use of the term, 'historical perspective' in the title of this paper, and the application of historical perspectives to contemporary educational issues (Aldrich 1996), also merit a brief explanation. History may be defined as the disciplined study of human events with particular reference to the dimension of time—principally in the past, but also with some acknowledgement of present and future. Such acknowledgement is essential, if only because that which is now past was once both a future and a present. Contemporary contests around the issue of educational standards frequently draw upon historical perspectives. For example, George Walden, a Conservative education minister, 1985–87 and columnist for the *Daily Telegraph*, has recently traced the perceived low standards of the English education system of today to the long-standing social class divide between private and state schools. Walden argues that while the seven per cent of children in private schools flourish, as indicated by levels of achievement in public examinations at ages 16 and 18, and by the 90 per cent of pupils from private schools who proceed to higher education, the remaining '93 per cent are still locked into a second-class system of education' (Walden 1996: 1). One major reason for this inferiority, according to Walden, is that teachers in private schools 'have remained largely immune to the social dogmas and experimental methods inflicted on generations of state school pupils' (Walden 1996: 44). Other commentators, however, including many teachers in state schools, would lay greater emphasis upon the link between educational standards and financial resources. Figures produced by Walden himself show the annual cost per secondary day pupil in state schools as being £2,250, with a pupil-teacher ratio of 18.4, as opposed to secondary day pupils in private schools with a cost of between £3,600 and £8,700 and a pupil-teacher ratio of 9.8 (Walden 1996: 43).

The journalist, Melanie Phillips, is another contemporary high-profile commentator on educational standards. Her book, *All Must Have Prizes*, also published in 1996, begins with a catalogue of evidence to demonstrate 'Standards sliding' (Phillips 1996: 1–6). Phillips, a columnist for the *Guardian*, *Observer* and *Sunday Times*, declares that today, 'The rot sets in at primary school level and runs throughout the system.' (Phillips 1996: 5) Her key chapter seven, entitled 'The Unravelling of the Culture', is historical. It traces 'the collapse of external authority that lies at the heart of the breakdown in education' (Phillips

1996: 187), from the Enlightenment and Rousseau, through a list of malign progressives which includes Holmes, Dewey, Nunn, Isaacs, Piaget, Simon and Stenhouse.

The belief that standards were better in the past has considerable nostalgic appeal and is frequently urged in the popular press. The following excerpts from the *Daily Mail* are typical: 'the brutal truth is that standards have fallen'; 'most parents and many teachers believe that children are less literate and numerate than they were 20 years ago'. From the opposite end of the political spectrum the *Daily Mirror* assures its readers that: 'literacy in Britain is marching backwards'; 'general educational standards have slipped alarmingly in the past decade or so' (Aldrich 1997: 9–10). These quotations, however, date from 1975 and 1976. Educational standards may, indeed, have fallen in the 1970s as in the 1990s, and in the 1980s as well, but due allowance must be made for the polemical style of many journalists, and for the well-attested fact that bad news sells more copies of newspapers (and of some books) than good.

Changes

Substantial changes in educational standards across time may be simply demonstrated. For example, in Britain, as in the western world in general, there was a general though uneven, rise in literacy levels across several centuries. Significant studies of such phenomena include those by Cipolla (1969), Clanchy (1979), Cressy (1980), Stephens (1987) and Vincent (1989). One important feature of these historical studies is their emphasis upon such factors as occupation and general culture in the increase (and occasional stagnation and decrease) in literacy levels. Thus Cressy notes that stagnation in the development of literacy during the second half of the eighteenth century has been associated by some historians with the 'social disruptions of the industrial revolution' (Cressy 1980: 177). Vincent explores the changing patterns of nineteenth-century male and female literacy, and highlights the contribution to literacy development of the penny post, and such associated features as Christmas and Valentine cards and the picture postcard. In 1858 'the Postmaster General had drawn attention to the fact that as many letters were being delivered in Manchester alone as in the whole of Russia' (Vincent 1989: 46).

Broad comparisons of literacy across centuries and cultures help to confirm the complex definitional problems associated with educational standards. In medieval Britain, education was construed primarily in vocational and religious contexts. Boys learned the skills of their fathers, and girls of their mothers; all were taught the basic elements of the Christian faith. Teaching and learning were essentially oral. The majority of people had neither the opportunity nor the immediate need to acquire literacy. Literacy, itself, is a term which is as difficult to define as to measure. The two skills of reading and writing have often been quite separate. In the early modern period, following the development of printing in the fifteenth century and the religious Reformation of the sixteenth, increasing numbers of people in Protestant countries learned to read the Bible and other religious works. This did not, however, necessarily mean that they also read secular literature, nor that they learned to write. The nature and extent of literacy (and numeracy) needed for an individual to function effectively in a particular society has clearly changed over time. Current debates about literacy levels should be set in a series of contexts which include the impact of such recent developments as the popular newspaper and typewriter in the nineteenth century, and television and the computer in the twentieth.

There is evidence to indicate that the steady improvement in literacy standards which took place across five centuries in Britain has not been maintained in the second half of the twentieth century. In a recent paper, presented at conferences in 1997, Greg Brooks of the National Foundation for Educational Research argues that during the period from 1948 until 1996 literacy standards in the United Kingdom changed very little. Indeed, there was a slight fall among eight year-olds (children in year 3) in England and Wales during the late 1980s, followed by a recovery in the early 1990s. This fall might have been associated with the introduction of the National Curriculum, which reduced the amount of time devoted to literacy in primary schools, and with the high number of teachers leaving the profession at that time. International evidence suggests that the levels achieved by high and middling performers in the United Kingdom are comparable to the best in the world, although among children and adults there is a significant proportion of the population who have poor literacy skills. Brooks concludes that the most effective way of raising average levels of achievement would be to 'intervene early in the education of children who are already failing or at risk of doing so, to ensure that they are equipped with the literacy (and numeracy) skills necessary for the rest of their education and for life' (Brooks 1997: 1).

First reports of a follow-up study to the ORACLE (Observational,

Research and Classroom Learning Evaluation) project, carried out in sixty East Midlands primary classrooms between 1976 and 1978, suggest not only stagnation, but actual decline. In July 1998, Maurice Galton reported in the *Times Educational Supplement* that his comparisons of children in years 4, 5 and 6 at the end of the school years 1976–7 and 1996–7 showed significant decline in the three basic areas of mathematics, reading and language skills. Galton judged that

> The fall appears to have occurred in the late 1980s and throughout the 1990s. The one factor which stands out in this period of rapid change is the national curriculum . . . Teachers said they were under pressure to get through the curriculum, emphasising instruction and content rather than teaching for understanding. . . . Teachers told us, despite denials from the Office for Standards in Education, that it is easier to pass inspections if you have a secondary-style timetable to demonstrate that the requisite hours are given to the core subjects. . . . It is perhaps ironic that those who have criticised primary teaching most vehemently, such as the Chief Inspector, helped to encourage this form of the national curriculum. (Galton 1998)

This evidence of stagnation or decline at primary levels in the 1980s and 1990s must be set against other evidence from the secondary, further and higher education sectors. Although commentators such as Phillips cite evidence of decline at all levels, there can be no doubt that over the same period there has been a steady increase in pupils achieving passes in public examinations at ages 16 and 18, while the numbers entering higher education and attaining degrees have more than doubled.

The Revised Code

In 1858 the Newcastle Commission was appointed to examine the condition of popular education in England. It reported in 1861. The Revd. James Fraser, an assistant commissioner, investigated elementary schooling in Devon, Dorset, Somerset, Herefordshire and Worcester. This substantial extract from his report indicates the religious, occupational, social class and gender contexts in which the most contentious example of government-directed attempts to raise educational standards took place.

> Even if it were possible, I doubt whether it would be desirable, with a view to the real interests of the peasant boy, to keep him at school till he was 14 or 15 years of age. But it is not possible. We must make up our minds to see the last of him, as far as the day school is concerned at 10 or 11. We must frame our system of education upon this hypothesis; and I venture to maintain that it is quite possible to teach a child soundly and thoroughly, in a way that he shall

not forget it, all that is necessary for him to possess in the shape of intellectual attainments by the time that he is 10 years old. If he has been properly
looked after in the lower classes, he shall be able to spell correctly the words
that he will ordinarily have to use; he shall read a common narrative—the
paragraph in the newspaper that he cares to read—with sufficient ease to be
a pleasure to himself and to convey information to listeners; if gone to live at
a distance from home, he shall write his mother a letter that shall be both
legible and intelligible; he knows enough of ciphering to make out, to test the
correctness of, a common shop bill; if he hears talk of foreign countries he
has some notions as to the part of the habitable globe in which they lie; and
underlying all, and not without its influence, I trust, upon his life and
conversation, he has acquaintance enough with the Holy Scriptures to follow
the allusions and the arguments of a plain Saxon sermon, and a sufficient
recollection of the truths taught him in his catechism, to know what are the
duties required of him towards his Maker and his fellow man. I have no
brighter view of the future or the possibilities of an English elementary
education, floating before my eyes than this. (Newcastle Report 1861: XXI
(ii) 46–7)

Not that Fraser believed that one half, or even a quarter of children
who left school aged 10 did 'carry with them into the business of life
even the humble amount of accomplishments which I have named. But
they ought to do; and in all the schools which in my list (Table XVIII) I
have named as "efficient" I believe they do.' (Newcastle Report 1861:
XXI (ii) 47)

Under the Revised Code of 1862 a large part of the central government's financial assistance to aided elementary schools was based upon
the principle of payment by results. Annual examinations were carried
out by Her Majesty's Inspectors, who were issued with detailed instructions for the purpose. Reading, and the slate work of younger children
in writing and arithmetic, were to be examined in the school. The paper
work of older scholars might be marked in the school, but all work done
on paper, together with the mark schedule, had to be sent to the
Education Department. The six standards established in 1862, which
roughly corresponded to children aged between six and 12 are shown in
Table 1.

A major Code revision occurred in 1872. The original Standard I
was abolished; the first examination of children would now normally
begin at age seven. The existing Standards II to VI were re-numbered I
to V. A new Standard VI was added, as shown in Table 2.

At the same time it was announced that henceforth no pupil could
be presented for examination for a second time under a lower standard
or for the same standard. Additionally, from 31 March 1873, no day

Table 1. Standards I–VI as established in 1862.

	Reading	Writing	Arithmetic
Standard I	Narrative in monosyllables.	Form on blackboard or slate from dictation, letters capital and small manuscript.	Form on blackboard or slate, from dictation, figures up to 20: name at sight figures up to 20: add and subtract figures up to 10, orally and from examples on the blackboard.
Standard II	One of the narratives next in order after monosyllables in an elementary reading book used in the school.	Copy in manuscript character a line of print.	A sum in simple addition and subtraction and the multiplication table.
Standard III	A short paragraph from an elementary reading book used in the school.	A sentence from the same paragraph, slowly read once and then dictated in single words.	A sum in any simple rule as far as short division (inclusive).
Standard IV	A short paragraph from a more advanced reading book used in the school.	A sentence slowly dictated once, by a few words at a time from the same book, but not from the paragraph read.	A sum in compound rules (money).
Standard V	A few lines of poetry from a reading book used in the first class in the school.	A sentence slowly dictated once, by a few words at a time, from a reading book used in the first class of the school.	A sum in compound rules (common weights and measures).
Standard VI	A short ordinary paragraph in a newspaper, or other modern narrative.	Another short ordinary paragraph in a newspaper, or other modern narrative, slowly dictated once by a few words at a time.	A sum in practice or bills of parcels.

Table 2. Standard VI from 1872.

Standard VI	To read with fluency and expression.	A short theme or letter, or an easy paraphrase.	Proportion and fractions (vulgar and decimal).

scholar over nine years of age and no evening scholar over 13 could be presented in Standard I, while from 31 March 1874 no day scholar over nine years of age, and no evening scholar above 14 could be presented for Standard II (CCE 1872: lxxxiii).

The results for England and Wales in the year ending 31 August 1872, the first year of the operation of the New Code, are shown in Table 3 (CCE 1873: xi-xii).

Comparison of standards during the period of payment by results is difficult. The addition of 'specific' subjects, which were examined individually, and 'class' subjects in which the overall proficiency of the class was assessed, provided other ways of securing grants. For example, in 1872 of the 118,799 children presented in Standards IV–VI, 71,507 were also examined in one or more of the specific subjects. Of these 49,273 secured passes, of whom 18,958 did so in two subjects, with geography, grammar and English history proving to be the most popular. The most obvious feature, however, was the large increase in the numbers of

Table 3.   Examination results for England and Wales in the year ending 31 August 1872.

Number of day scholars qualified for examination	792,706
Number presented for examination	661,589
Number presented in Standard I	258,946
Number presented in Standard II	172,391
Number presented in Standard III	111,453
Number presented in Standard IV	66,925
Number presented in Standard V	36,843
Number presented in Standard VI	15,031
Number examined under 10 years of age	342,655
Number examined over 10 years of age	318,934
Number examined in Standards I–III	
Under 10 years of age	339,618
Over 10 years of age	203,172
Number examined in Standards IV–VI	
Under 10 years of age	3,037
Over 10 years of age	115,762
Number who passed without failure in any subject	
Standards I–III	
Under 10 years of age	213,395
Over 10 years of age	122,704
Standards IV–VI	
Under 10 years of age	1,814
Over 10 years of age	63,982

schools seeking government recognition as public elementary schools for the purposes of obtaining grants. The New Code was introduced in the immediate aftermath of the Elementary Education Act of 1870 which established school boards empowered to levy a rate for education. In consequence, whereas in the period 1862 to 1869 the average number of schools seeking inspection for the purposes of obtaining grants was 492, in 1870 the figure was 1,114 and in 1872, 1,530. The annual report of the Committee of Council on Education for 1872–3 welcomed the increase in applications, and thus in scholars presented for examination. But it also regretted the considerable numbers of scholars who were not entered for any examinations, the great preponderance of scholars in Standards I–III as opposed to IV–VI, and the very high percentage of those aged 10 or over who were presented in Standards I–III.

Joseph Payne, a former schoolmaster who in 1873 became first professor of the College of Preceptors, was one of the major critics of standards under the system of payment by results (Aldrich 1995: 179–85). In September 1872 he presented a paper entitled 'Why are the results of our primary instruction so unsatisfactory?' to the annual congress of the Social Science Association in Plymouth. The tone of his paper was calculated to shock: 'This, then, is the final result of the working of 15,000 schools, conducted by 26,000 teachers, at a cost of about one million a year. All this stupendous machinery is contrived and kept in motion to send out into the world annually about 16,000 children with the ability to read, write and cipher moderately well' (Payne 1872: 245).

Another opponent was John Menet, Vicar of Hockerill, whose 26-page pamphlet, *A Letter to a Friend on the Standards of the New Code of the Education Department*, was published in 1874. In this work Menet posed the question 'Why, then, is the principle of Standards radically bad?' (Menet 1874: 7) and grouped his answers under eight main themes.

The first was that it was impossible to devise standards for the whole country. No two schools were alike. Some were established and settled, others were new and reliant on shifting populations. Some were large with children classified according to standards, others had all pupils in the one class. Some children walked to school along a few yards of pavement, others trudged for hours across muddy field, moorland or fen. Given the variety of school circumstances it was obvious that a single set of standards would be much too difficult for some and much too easy for others.

The second problem was that the minimum requirements laid down by the standards too often became the maximum. If a penalty was imposed for not reaching a particular level, then the chief aim was to avoid the penalty, and not to aspire to anything much beyond it. The grudging spirit in which the Code was operated was indicated by the instructions to inspectors issued from the Council Office in September 1862. These advised that inspectors must be satisfied as before on a range of matters—including the state of the buildings, qualifications of the teachers, and keeping of registers—and that the new examination would not supersede judgments in these matters but rather presuppose them. The examination results did not prescribe that '*if thus much is done, a grant shall be paid*, but, *unless thus much is done, no grant shall be paid*' (CCE 1863: xviii).

Menet's third point was the effect of standards on the quicker and slower children. Quicker children were held back, for there was a serious disadvantage to the school in children passing through the standards too quickly. One standard per year was the most they should progress in order to get the maximum grant. On the other hand, the slowest children could not keep up with the rate of one standard per year. It was for this reason that so many children were presented in the lower standards, and some not at all. From a financial point of view, schools had every inducement to neglect children who had little or no chance of being successful.

His fourth criticism, and that which was most frequently made against the system, was that standards encouraged a dull and mechanical routine of teaching and learning. In 1872 Payne had complained that the system of payment by results was 'mechanical in conception, mechanical in means, mechanical in results . . . Making quantity not quality the test of your results, you shall fail in securing either quantity or quality. The experiment which has now been tried for ten years in England ought henceforth to take a place in the annals of education as an example to deter.' (Payne 1872: 247–8) As HMI Kennedy acknowledged in his report for 1872, under the aegis of standards, most elementary schools merely became glorified infant schools in which nothing but reading, writing and arithmetic were taught at increasing levels of complexity. Such a curriculum stifled true mental progress and development. The teacher's task became to secure as many passes as possible. One of the most telling sections in Menet's pamphlet was his use of quotations from such experienced inspectors as Arnold, Campbell, Fussell, Kennedy, Mitchell, Stewart and Watkins, all of whom contrasted the superior teaching and learning that went on in many schools before the introduction of the Revised Code. For example, Matthew Arnold was quoted from his report for 1872–3: 'I have never concealed from your Lordships that our mode of payment by results, as it is called, puts in the way of the good teaching and the good learning of these subjects almost insuperable obstacles' (Menet 1874: 13).

The next criticism concerned the increasingly mercenary approach to education engendered in school managers and teachers. By the end of the 1860s the term, 'farming of schools', was widely used in inspectors' and other official reports. Children were seen not as individuals or as learners, but as grant-earners. In some schools the teacher's salary was based directly upon the number of passes and grant earned. Indeed, in some cases, Menet reported, 'the commercial element is still further strengthened by the return of a certain amount in some shape to the children who pass in the Standards' (Menet 1874: 17).

Standards also interfered with the organisation of a school. In Menet's view, schools should be organised by classes, not by standards. Children should be grouped according to their educational needs, not according to grant-earning requirements. He also asked why standards and payment by results should be applied only to public elementary schools, but not to middle-class, private, grammar or public schools? What would a parent say to a master or mistress in one of these schools who announced that children would be limited to a narrow curriculum, not allowed to progress too quickly through that curriculum, and that only selected scholars who were likely to pass would be entered for the annual examination? Finally, Menet criticised 'the disastrous effects of the Standards . . . upon Inspection properly so called, as distinguished from mere Examination' (Menet 1874: 19).

Menet's solutions were based upon the abolition of the system of standards, and its replacement by a return to an annual examination by properly trained inspectors, 'an examination which would be fairly within the range of each school, according to its circumstances and standing' (Menet 1874: 23). He concluded:

> We want, on the one hand, less routine, less mechanism, less complication, fewer pains and penalties. We want in their place, on the other hand, a much fuller and clearer recognition of what Education really is, more freedom for Inspectors, more liberty for Teachers, more cultivation of mind, and more common sense. Let the weights be removed which press on all sides, and everybody concerned will breathe more freely. (Menet 1874: 26)

The criticisms of Menet and Payne, among others, did not go entirely unheeded. The system which they deplored was further modified, for example, by the addition of a seventh standard in 1882. In the same year, the Education Department's instructions to inspectors allowed them to calculate part of the grant upon 'the estimate you form of the merit of the school as a whole' (CCE 1883: 157). Although the quantity and quality of the pupils' passes were still to be the major factors in such an estimate, some allowance could also be made for 'special circumstances', for example 'a shifting, scattered, very poor or ignorant population' (CCE 1883: 157).

Payment by results came to an end in the last decade of the nineteenth century, but the concept and terminology of standards with which it had been associated, lasted into the twentieth. The very standards themselves, in tabular form, continued to be included in the elementary school code. In 1912 John Adams, first principal of the London Day Training College, delivered a presidential address entitled 'An objective standard in education' to the Educational Science section at the Dundee meeting of the British Association. In this address, and in his major work, *The Evolution of Educational Theory*, first published in the same year, Adams showed how the old concept of standards had so passed into common usage that people talked about children not as being of a certain age, or ability, but as 'being in standard so-and-so' (Adams 1912: 304). Adams gave a cautious welcome to the work of Binet and Simon in respect of intelligence scales, for, as he observed, standards, which had been 'Primarily meant as means of measuring the money value of the communication of certain bits of information . . . came in the teacher's hands to be a means of estimating ability' (Adams 1912: 304).

Conclusions

Four broad conclusions may be drawn.

The first is that the term, 'standards', has occupied a prominent and contested place in recent British educational history. This is not surprising, given the ever-changing nature and amount of knowledge, coupled with changes in educational and broader societal priorities. It is not difficult to dip into that history to find evidence for, or against, a decline in standards over time. On the one hand it is clear that literacy standards are higher in the twentieth century than in any previous period. Similarly, a much greater percentage of the population now attends university and is educated to degree level than ever before. In the middle years of the twentieth century grammar schooling was deemed to be appropriate for twenty per cent of the population. Today thirty per cent enter higher education. Improved educational access and standards have been particularly visible in respect of females. Not until the nineteenth century did female literacy begin to equal that of males, nor women gain access to higher education. On the other hand, there can be little doubt that levels of attainment in some subjects were higher in the later nineteenth century than they are today. For example, it seems likely that: more children knew the Lord's Prayer, Creed and Catechism than today; more boys could work complex sums in multiplication and long division; more girls were skilled in needlework; more children could recite substantial amounts of poetry. Some of these accomplishments were the direct product of the system of standards. Under the Code of 1883, when English was taken as a class subject children in Standard I were required to 'repeat 20 lines of simple verse'. This was followed by '40 lines of poetry' with associated tasks for Standard II, 60 for III, 80 for IV, and 100 for V. Standard VI children had 'To recite 150 lines from Shakespeare or Milton, or some other standard author, and to explain the words and allusions' (CCE 1883: 132–3). It is not difficult to gather such evidence about rising or falling standards. What is more difficult, but considerably more worthwhile, is to situate and evaluate it in the context of the time, and in historical perspective.

The standards debate of the second half of the nineteenth century took place in a series of contexts which in some respects were quite different from those of today. But although there are differences, similarities are also apparent. The Revised Code was introduced in 1862, not in implementation of the major recommendation of the Newcastle Report, which called for the introduction of a local system of county boards and local inspectors, but to avoid it. Not until 1870 would local boards be allowed to intrude into the field of public education. In 1862 teachers, who in the eyes of the government had been getting above themselves, would immediately be brought to account by the introduction of 'a little free trade'. Payment by results, it was argued, meant that, in future, government and taxpayers would get better value for money. Elementary education would either be efficient or it would be cheap. But was elementary education made more efficient? Menet's most persuasive argument against the system of standards of his day was that many of the HMIs who operated the assessment regime upon which payment by results was based, were prepared to state publicly that, on balance, it was harmful to good teaching and learning. They, and Menet himself, while fully committed to the need for some form of externally-based assessment, concluded that such assessment must be professional and formative as well as managerial and summative.

Evidence from the other side of the world lends support to this conclusion. For in New Zealand from 1877 an almost identical system applied. Its central features—a national syllabus divided into prescribed standards, school inspectors whose role was to apply the assessment system and take no responsibility for its effects—were essentially the same, although without the direct operation of payment by results. In New Zealand, school examination results were published in tabulated form in newspapers, and in 1880 the government declared that 'the school with the lowest average age and the highest percentage of passes in the same standards is the most efficient . . . . a high average age and a low percentage of passes indicates a school of the opposite character' (McKenzie 1994: 249). David McKenzie has recently concluded that the system of external review based upon standards as operated in New Zealand, even without the dimension of payment by results, was essentially miseducative. The initiatives of better teachers were curbed; weaker teachers taught to the test and some engaged in outright dishonesty. Intended minima soon became maxima; good teaching and educational improvement were stifled. McKenzie supports Matthew Arnold's identification of the underlying problem, namely that the fault lay in the bureaucratic system of evaluation itself, rather than in its specific use for the purpose of payment by results (McKenzie 1994: 251). McKenzie drew upon this historical perspective to argue that criticisms of the Education Review Office in New Zealand 'owe their origin to the failure of the Picot Committee to grasp that a distanced review authority which is required to act judgmentally will be unable to facilitate the co-operative activity that the process of educational review requires' (McKenzie 1994: 247).

The third point concerns the contributions which historians can make in relation to educational research. In 1996, in a lecture entitled 'Teaching as a research-based profession: possibilities and prospects', David Hargreaves argued that much educational research, unlike that in medicine or the natural sciences, was 'non-cumulative, in part because few researchers seek to create a body of knowledge which is then tested, extended or replaced in some systematic way' (Hargreaves 1996: 2). The historian can employ a chronological approach to provide a cumulative account, but must also indicate some of the difficulties inherent in creating, testing, extending or replacing bodies of knowledge in educational research. There are continuities in educational history, and it is not difficult to show, for example, that some basic principles of teaching and learning have as much validity in the twentieth century as in the nineteenth. Progress in some matters—for example, better physical health and improved literacy rates—can also be demonstrated over long periods of time. But it is difficult to be prescriptive about all issues of educational practice, and to measure progress (or decline) in all areas, including overall educational standards, essentially because the concept of education (like that of progress) is not value-free. Education, indeed, has been well defined as initiation into worthwhile activities, and it is clear that assessments of what knowledge (and of what standards) are of most worth, have been, and will continue to be, matters of debate. It seems probable that one of the best means of ensuring improvements in educational standards is for that debate to be conducted in a constructive and co-operative way.

Finally, it is important to end on a positive note. The current government's commitment to the raising of educational standards is to be welcomed, as are many of its initiatives to achieve this aim, particularly the establishment of General Teaching Councils for England and Wales. Central government should continue to do what it can to contribute towards the raising of standards. But it should also recognize both the limitations of its own role, and that pupils, parents, teachers, local authorities and others have most significant parts to play.

Education is not susceptible to quick fixes, whether as a result of political intervention or pedagogical fashion. Teaching is not like some other professions, for example medicine and the law, where high profile and dramatic results may be easily and quickly achieved. The two fundamental factors in raising educational standards are the steady commitment to worthwhile education amongst pupils, parents and society at large, and the recruitment and retention of as many good teachers as possible.

This paper ends, as it began, with definitions. Worthwhile education is about the promotion of knowledge over ignorance, of truth over falsehood, of concern for others over selfishness, over effort over sloth, of mental and physical well-being over despair and debility. If we neglect these truths in order to put a spin or gloss upon education for other purposes—whether we are politicians, journalists, authors, academics, teachers—then we shall be agents in lowering rather than raising educational standards. Good teachers may be defined as those with a sound knowledge of their subjects and of pedagogy, steady application of principles of management and organization, genuine concern for those whom they teach, and the ability to inspire and enthuse.

Discussion

Gillian Sutherland

Definitions

Richard Aldrich has rightly drawn attention to the range and elaboration of definitions of standards in the *Oxford English Dictionary*. The most relevant for an analysis of the appeals to standards in England over the last two centuries are those under the general heading II: 'Exemplar, measure of weight'. Sub-set 12 reads: 'A definite level of excellence, attainment, wealth or the like, or a definite degree of any quality, viewed as a prescribed object of endeavour or as the measure of what is adequate for some purpose.' The words 'prescribed' and 'adequate for some purpose' are deserving of emphasis: reminders that the aim must always be to reach behind the immediate appeal to standards and ask, 'for what purpose?' This must be an over-arching objective and a recurring theme in any extended discussion.

With this proviso, these dictionary definitions offer two linked but distinct notions. The first is that of a target of endeavour, a level of excellence, which only a few will reach. The second is that of a measure of what is adequate, a minimum acceptable level which almost everyone is able to reach. Between excellence and adequacy there may be a large gap. These two notions are nevertheless of considerable help in disentangling the various forms that invocation of standards took in the educational discourse of nineteenth century England. Such invocations were always linked to formal examinations, a mechanism embraced with passion by nineteenth-century educational activists; but formal examinations were conducted for a variety of objectives. The first wave of enthusiasm for examinations was part of a project to identify and reward elites: standards were a measure of excellence. Only later, as schemes for mass education gained momentum, were examinations used and standards invoked to measure adequacy.

Nineteenth-century Discussions

(1) Excellence and Elites

The use of formal examinations to set a target of excellence which only a few would attain but representing a pinnacle against which others could measure themselves, gathered momentum in the universities of Oxford and Cambridge from the 1780s onward. By the end of the 1820s it was well-established, a model for other universities and being brandished as the tool to overhaul selection for the Indian Civil Service. Macaulay spoke eloquently in favour of using competitive examination to this end in the House of Commons in 1833 (Macaulay 1898: xi, 571–3). He justified his position in these terms:

> Education would be mere useless torture, if, at two or three and twenty, a man who had neglected his studies were exactly on a par with a man who had applied himself to them, exactly as likely to perform all the offices of public life with credit to himself and with advantage to society. Whether the English system of education be good or bad is not now the question. Perhaps I may think that too much time is given to the ancient languages and to the abstract sciences. But what then? Whatever be the languages, whatever be the sciences, which it is, in any age or country, the fashion to teach, the persons who will become the greatest proficients in those languages and those sciences will generally be the flower of the youth, the most acute, the most industrious, the most ambitious of honourable distinctions.

It took twenty years to replace patronage by competitive examination. However the experience was one on which Macaulay's brother-in-law, Charles Trevelyan, was able to draw when he was then asked to turn his attention to the Home Civil Service (Sutherland 1984: 97–100). By this time too examinations were being deployed to stir up moribund grammar school foundations and to assess the work of the new proprietary boarding schools. There was a bandwagon rolling on which women as well as men would climb in the second half of the century (Roach 1971, Fletcher 1980).

When the notion of a standard was invoked in such discussions it was almost always seen as an absolute, an external fixed reference point. In the University of Oxford a committee of the Hebdomadal Board, appointed in March 1829 to construct a new Examination Statute, saw their objective to be the creation of a self-activating mechanism to stimulate both teaching and study and reaffirmed that 'the standard for each class be absolute and positive' (Brock and Curthoys 1998: 344). Theoretically all the candidates could be in the first class and individual classes could be empty; as, in subsequent years, they sometimes were. Those concerned with the technology of assessment in the late twentieth century would recognize an early example of criterion referencing. The criteria constructed in such examinations, moreover, trailed an aura of enormous power. Macaulay had made an explicit equation of ability and merit; and this equation was deployed enthusiastically and effectively by his supporters and successors (Sutherland 1984: 97–113, Young 1958).

(2) *Adequacy and Mass Schooling*

Developing from mid-century, side by side with but distinct from the invocation of excellence, was the invocation of a standard as a measure of adequacy, an acceptable minimum floor, which almost everyone was expected to achieve. Again examinations were the chosen mechanism and this is the discourse to which the Revised Code of 1862 and payment by results, explored at length by Aldrich, belonged.

Some of the immediate power and impact of the Revised Code and its examination Standards came from the fact that real money depended on them. For the thirty years of its operation the bulk of the government grant to a school—over half its annual income—depended on the children's passes in these Standards; and many managers tightened the link by making some fraction of the teacher's salary dependent on the pass rate achieved. Such acts dramatize the close connections between the Revised Code and the conceptual framework of free market economics.

(3) *The Market Model*

Robert Lowe, the Revised Code's principal architect, saw government as the consumer of mass education, getting—or failing to get—value for money in the form of certain minimum skill levels. He expounded his thinking in the House of Commons in February 1862 (*Hansard* 3rd ser. 13 February 1862: 205):

> What is the object of inspection? Is it simply to make things pleasant, give the schools as much as can be got out of the public purse, independent of their efficiency; or do you mean that our grants should not only be aids, subsidies and gifts, but fruitful of good? That is the question and it meets us at every

turn. Are you for efficiency or for a subsidy? Is a school to be relieved because it is bad and therefore poor, or because it is a good school and therefore efficient and in good circumstances?

The use of the market as a model for educational provision was sharply challenged by one of Lowe's own inspectors, Matthew Arnold. After an initial challenge to the Revised Code itself, Arnold drew back: he could not afford to lose his job. He inspected, grumbling, under its rules for the remainder of his career (Sutherland 1973b: 12–13). However in writing about secondary education—his real passion and an area for which the state as yet took no responsibility—Arnold tackled the model of the market head on. In *A French Eton* in 1863 he proclaimed 'that to trust to the principle of supply and demand to do for us all that we want in providing education is to lean upon a broken reed' (Arnold 1863: 282). He continued:

> The mass of mankind know good butter from bad, and tainted meat from fresh, and the principle of supply and demand may, perhaps, be relied upon to give us sound meat and butter. But the mass of mankind do not so well know what distinguishes good teaching and training from bad; they do not here know what they ought to demand, and, therefore, the demand cannot be relied on to give us the right supply. Even if they knew what they ought to demand, they have no sufficient means of testing whether or no this is really supplied to them.

At this point Arnold was primarily concerned to challenge the idea that either pupils seeking education or their parents ought to be seen as consumers or customers. He went on, however, to argue that neither was the state a consumer or customer in the simple and straightforward sense that Lowe had posited. Rather, the state was pupils, parents, all citizens, in their collective and corporate character. Deliberately Arnold echoed Burke in seeing 'the citizens of a State, the members of a society' as a partnership, 'a partnership in all science, in all art, in every virtue, in all perfection'. Viewed from this standpoint, the provision of national education became for Arnold both more complex and a project of fundamental moral importance: one for which the model and language of the market were wholly inappropriate.

(4) *Standards and Averages*

Although the grant and inspection arrangements embodied in the Revised Code were dismantled in the 1890s, many of the habits and patterns formed by it persisted far longer. The teaching habits developed to survive within it died hard, as did the firm classification of children by age and the physical structures developed to accommodate this grouping. How many readers of this note attended a primary school which labelled its classes—sometimes had incised above its doors—Standards I, II, III etc.? For the Revised Code had determined grant awards during the years of massive school building immediately following the 1870 Act.

Further, while 'Standard', remaining a class label, ceased to be an examination, the idea of a standard as a measure of adequacy was given fresh power and tied closely to the term 'average' by the work of Francis Galton. In his *Hereditary Genius* in 1869 and subsequently he argued that human abilities were distributed along a normal bell-shaped curve. Thus there would be a small number whose abilities and achievements were exceptional—excellent—and a small number whose abilities and achievements would be abysmal, while the abilities and achievements of the majority clustered around the middle ranks, the average (Mackenzie 1981: 56–8). Effective testing and examining could therefore be expected to spread candidates in the familiar bell-shaped pattern: a handful at each extreme, the majority bunched in the middle.

This assumption was fundamental to the subsequent development of group mental, or as they came to be called, intelligence tests and of standardized tests of attainments (Sutherland 1984: 115–27). Like the tests of the Revised Code, these are tests for ordering large populations and were used as such in secondary school selection in England from the 1920s onwards (Sutherland 1984: 164–269, Thom 1986: 117–23). Standards in this discourse were what technologists of assessment would call norm referenced, shaped by the pattern of performance of the majority. Yet at the same time the assumption that human abilities follow the normal curve of distribution made it easy to bring measures of excellence and measures of adequacy into a close linear relationship.

The Continuing Resonances of Past Debates

Richard Aldrich has noted some of the criticisms of payment by results made at the time. These could be extensively amplified from the reports of other inspectors (e.g. Sutherland 1973: 195–7) and from the comments of a later chief inspector, Edmond Holmes, on the revelation it was to him when payment by results came to an end. His lament that the methods of teaching and examining reading created a culture in which children left school never having learnt to use books (Holmes 1911: 127), has an extraordinarily contemporary ring. Worries of the 1990s about the costs and administrative burden of an elaborate apparatus of national assessment evoke powerful echoes of the infighting within the Civil Service in the 1880s over precisely such issues—and this infighting was one factor contributing to the destruction of payment by results (Sutherland 1973: 237–45).

Exact analogies, however, are always difficult to sustain and comparisons forward are dangerously a-historical. An intellectual tactic which is more respectable and robust than such comparisons is to treat the nineteenth century's invocation of 'standards' as a piece of vicarious experience. This prompts several questions which seem pertinent for the late twentieth century debate. Are standards understood to be the target of excellence, which only the few can attain, although they may define and rank the lesser achievements of the many? Or are they meant to be the minimum acceptable floor for almost everyone? Or does popular discourse slither in confused fashion back and forth between these two poles? Has an average now become this minimum acceptable floor, something everyone must achieve, detached from any conceptual relation it once had to a normal curve of distribution? These seem appropriate questions to ask when a successor to Edmond Holmes heads the Office for Standards in Education; and when publication of A level results, GCSE results and primary school league tables generates regular media feeding frenzies.

Finally we should return to questions of purpose. What models are the appropriate ones to apply to the provision of education? This seems a pertinent question when the possibility of handing over schools, both 'failing' and functioning, to entrepreneurs begins to be canvassed (e.g. Davis 1993). Whenever the cry of 'standards' is invoked, the supporting agenda must be explored too.

Anthony Heath

I enjoyed Aldrich's paper and learned a great deal from it, particularly about the Revised Code which clearly has intriguing parallels with contemporary attempts to secure better value for money in education.

Aldrich makes a crucial distinction between the notion of a standard as a yardstick for judging performance and a standard in the sense of the average level of attainment as measured by that yardstick. While there is bound to be considerable uncertainty about the equivalence of the yardsticks used in different periods, there seems little doubt that there has been historically a substantial improvement in the educational attainments of the British population, at least in the sense that larger proportions of the population have acquired basic literacy and formal qualifications. Of course in this respect Britain is no different from other industrialised countries (see for example Blossfeld and Shavit 1993).

Aldrich describes a steady improvement in literacy across five centuries in Britain, although this improvement has not perhaps been maintained in the second half of the twentieth century. However, lack of recent progress on raising standards, that is the lack of growth in the proportion of the age-group reaching a basic level of literacy, has perhaps been compensated for by increasing proportions reaching higher levels of educational attainment such as GCSE, A level and degree.

This can be illustrated with data from the General Household Surveys. The GHS collects data on respondents' highest educational qualifications, and we can arrange these data by the respondents' years of birth. Arranged in this way the GHS data give a picture of the growth over the course of the twentieth century in the proportions from successive birth cohorts who have acquired educational qualifications. (Since people can go on acquiring qualifications throughout the life cycle, these cohort differences almost certainly underestimate the true changes in the qualifications of the population at the time they left full-time education.)

As we can see, the percentage with no formal educational qualification fell from 73% of men and 86% of women in the oldest birth cohort, born in the years 1900–09, to 12% of men and 16% of women in the youngest cohort, born seventy years later. Perhaps the most striking increases are in the percentages with intermediate qualifications such as A or O level (and their historical equivalents). The increases at these levels have been substantially greater than those at the highest qualification levels such as degree.[1]

If we take basic literacy as the lowest level of attainment, as Aldrich notes, 'take-off' occurred in the nineteenth century or earlier, and began to approach a ceiling in the second half of the twentieth century. The next expansion, as shown in Table 1, was in intermediate secondary qualifications which 'took off' much later, in the second half of the twentieth century, and may be expected to reach their ceiling early in the twenty-first century. A third expansion, in tertiary education, has only recently begun and it is too early to say when and at what level a ceiling will be reached.

Table 1. Highest qualification by cohort for males and females (%)

	1900–09	1910–19	1920–29	1930–39	1940–49	1950–59	1960–69	1970–79
Males								
Degree	3.0	4.0	5.9	7.7	10.5	12.6	11.5	9.4
Higher: below degree	2.9	3.7	5.7	7.6	10.5	12.1	12.0	11.5
A level	1.4	2.1	3.0	5.8	9.7	16.4	18.3	30.9
O level	3.8	5.7	6.7	11.1	15.9	20.0	26.5	27.3
Low	16.2	17.9	18.3	18.4	14.0	10.6	14.1	8.6
None	72.8	66.6	60.3	49.3	39.4	28.4	17.6	12.2
N	3101	15900	29444	29334	35284	33945	21441	3949
Females								
Degree	.9	.9	1.4	2.4	4.0	6.9	8.7	11.4
Higher: Below degree	3.2	4.3	5.2	7.9	8.8	10.1	8.3	5.4
A level	.8	.7	1.0	2.0	3.8	7.7	12.1	16.8
O level	2.6	4.1	6.4	10.4	16.8	25.4	36.4	38.9
Low	6.4	9.1	11.7	13.7	16.6	14.5	16.4	11.4
None	86.2	80.9	74.4	63.6	50.0	35.5	18.1	16.1
N	3866	19440	33259	31655	38371	36881	23185	4156

Notes.
1. To maximize the reliability and time-span of the estimates we have cumulated General Household Surveys for the years 1973 to 1992. We restrict table 1 to respondents aged 21 and over at the time of the survey in which they were interviewed.
2. The decline in the youngest birth cohorts in the proportions obtaining a degree reflects the fact that degrees are typically obtained at older ages and that some members of these younger cohorts had not yet finished their education.

In describing the trends in attainment over the twentieth century, it must be recognised that we cannot make any claims to exact equivalence in the yardsticks used. While in some cases, such as degrees, there has been some institutional continuity at least in the title of the qualification, in others there have been major reorganisations. For example, school Certificate and Higher School Certificate were replaced by GCE O and A level; the new qualification of CSE was introduced and then amalgamated with O level to form the GCSE. There are conventions about what count as equivalent: for example, a pass at school certificate is taken to be equivalent to an O level at grades 1–5 or, subsequently, at grades A–C; CSE grade 1 and GCSE at grades A–C are assumed to be the more recent equivalents. All can be regarded as intermediate secondary qualifications taken at around age 15/16.

We certainly could not claim that this convention provides exact equivalence. It is quite possible to argue that in some sense a grade C at GCSE today is at a lower standard than a grade C at O level and that the yardstick has in this way been debased. Some of the growth in the percentages gaining O level equivalents, as shown in table 1, might thus be accounted for by the 'standards' becoming easier. On the other hand we would want to claim that this convention is better than most alternative conventions: it would make even less sense to treat *any* pass at O level and GCSE as equivalent irrespective of the grade obtained. In other words, the convention being used is probably the least bad of the possible conventions, but certainly falls short of the ideal (although the exact nature of the ideal may itself be unknowable). Moreover, I doubt if anyone would wish to argue that the whole of the increase in attainments shown in Table 1 could be explained by debasement of the yardstick. Indeed, if we adopted a more conservative convention and claimed that a contemporary A level is of the same standard as the pre-war school certificate, the GHS data would still show a huge increase in attainment.

Of course, failure to maintain comparable yardsticks over time is a serious handicap for sociologists who wish to determine whether social class, gender or ethnic inequalities in attainment have been reduced over time or who wish to monitor the effectiveness of government education policy (see for example Heath and Clifford 1990). If our yardstick changes, it becomes difficult to provide definitive answers to our research questions. But as Jencks once remarked 'We are aware of the hazards involved and have tried to check the validity of our assumptions wherever possible. Nonetheless, the methods we have used may involve considerable error. In self-defence, we can only say that the magnitude of these errors is almost certainly less than if we had simply consulted our prejudices, which seems to be the usual alternative' (Jencks 1972: 15).

But should we even expect the yardstick to remain the same over time? As Aldrich argues, the societal functions have changed over time and there may be good educational reasons for the changing nature of the yardsticks used. One function, although not perhaps the only one, is that these qualifications are used as a selection device by, for example, schools, universities and to a lesser extent employers.

However, as secondary education has expanded and more students stay on to take the public examinations at age sixteen, so the purpose of the selection has also changed. Thus pre-war, when very few pupils stayed on at secondary school beyond the minimum leaving age (which was then fourteen), school certificate and matriculation were geared to University entrance. After the war, as increasing numbers stayed on at school, O levels became a prerequisite for access to A level courses in the sixth form. After the raising of the school-leaving age in 1973/4 O level, CSE and now GCSE had to cater for the whole ability range and began to function as a school-leaving certificate for many pupils. Given the huge changes in numbers staying on at school and taking these examinations, and given the very different 'gate-keeper' roles that these examinations performed, it would be extraordinary if they had maintained the same 'standards' over time. And it would probably have been quite inappropriate if they had done so: a yardstick that would have been a good discriminator between borderline candidates for university admission before the war is unlikely to be a good discriminator for borderline candidates for entry to the sixth form after the war or for entry to skilled occupations at the end of the century.

Given the historical transformation of our educational system, therefore, and the changing selective functions which the public examinations have been asked to perform, it is highly desirable that the yardstick should be changed from time to time so that it is appropriate for its current function. If what we want is a selection device, then we need something that is a good discriminator at the borderline. As the borderline changes, so should the yardstick.

Public examinations are a central component of a meritocratic selection procedure for selecting young people for post-school entry to colleges or employment. It follows that their primary purpose should be to secure equity between current applicants for entry rather than between generations. Rather than debating whether yardsticks have been debased over time, it is more useful to consider whether current examination procedures are adequately designed for the selection functions they are currently asked to perform.

Acknowledgements

I would like to thank the Office of National Statistics and the Data Archive at the University of Essex for making the General Household Survey data available. I am very grateful to Jane Roberts at the Social Studies Computing Unit, Oxford, for her work on cumulating the files.

Sig Prais

The specification of schooling standards on a *nationwide* basis is not something newly devised in the past decade for the National Curriculum in this country. Richard Aldrich has reminded us in his paper, that it can be traced back to the middle of the last century in relation to core subjects. I should like to offer some comments on what we mean, or should mean, when we talk of educational standards. The clarification of a number of complex associated issues, I shall suggest, would do much to improve rational policy formation. My comments will focus on the gap between specified standards and pupils' actual attainments, the meaning of expected standards and the care needed in measuring pupils at the lower end of the achievement spectrum.

First, the gap between specified *standards* and pupils' actual *attainments* is important. For example, does a teacher concentrate on bringing more marginal low-attaining children across a lower boundary (as under the English nineteenth century payment-by-results system), or does she concentrate on the highest attaining children, to bring more up to those higher standards on which her success—and that of her school—may be assessed, as in the days of the 11–plus and scholarship examinations? That difference in teaching emphasis is well-recognised.

Secondly, expectations: when government policy speaks of the educational 'standards of 11 year-olds *expected* for their age' we need to be very clear as to what is meant by 'expected'. Statisticians use the term 'expectation' to mean simply the arithmetic average, without any moral or policy implications: a statistician might say that the 'expected' height of a grown man in England is 5 foot 7 inches. There is no necessary implication that those below the average could or should be raised to that 'expectation' by a series of policies, even if that were possible. If educational policies now aim to raise 80 per cent of pupils, as is said, to the 'standards expected for their age', it is probably most reasonable to interpret this as meaning that at some future date the top 80 per cent of pupils will reach the attainments that the middle pupil happens to reach today.

To require 80 per cent of children to reach standards in literacy and numeracy hitherto attained only by 50 per cent seems likely to require a great shift in school time-tables towards those subjects (English and mathematics), and away from other subjects, together with reforms in syllabuses, teaching methods and classroom organisation. Some of those reforms are under way in the new Labour Government's policy recommendations for primary schools for a daily Literacy Hour and a Numeracy Hour; but prudent observers will hold their breath as to whether present and planned reforms in teaching methods and classroom organisation will go far enough to achieve the stated aims.

In moving the focus of official educational policy towards pupils at the lower part of the attainment range, we may detect a belated recognition of the view that paramount importance in current schooling reforms attaches to the *employment* consequences of continuing advances of automation and computerisation throughout the economy. The increased demand for personnel to serve as highly skilled technicians has long been clear; but of equal economic significance, and probably of greater social significance, is the decline in employability of that great proportion of school-leavers who previously were provided with schooling which led only to unskilled work.

An associated worry arises from the spread of new styles of teaching which incorporate a greater degree of 'discovery learning' by the pupil— such as, learning to read by recognising the length and shape of whole words rather than how sounds are represented by letters ('look-and-say' versus 'phonics'), or relying on a calculator at early ages rather than embedding arithmetical bonds in the mind (Bierhoff 1996: 152). There is space here only to adumbrate the complexities at issue: it is possible that these new methods may work well with high-ability children (the methods were often developed in 'model schools' attached to universities, attended by professors' children with all the help that such children have at home at their disposal); but they may have done a great disservice to children from problem homes who rely to a greater extent on their teachers for guidance, and require a stable classroom environment for emotional security as a pre-condition for efficient learning. The new teaching methods may thus have done both some good and some harm; irrespective of whether the *average* has slightly risen or slightly fallen, we need to have our eye on the *spread* of attainments a matter to which educational researchers have given little attention. The great worry is that, in an era when technological developments in the economy have reduced employment opportunities for children of below-average attainments, developments in teaching may have served to reduce their opportunities yet further.

The Role of Public Examinations in Defining and Monitoring Standards

MIKE CRESSWELL

Examination Standards and Educational Standards

I INTERPRET THE PHRASE *educational standards,* in its widest sense, to mean the quality of educational provision and I take it that interest in the monitoring of such standards is motivated by a desire for valid information upon which to base policies intended to improve that quality. Despite being concerned only with some of the objectives of education, public examinations play a major role in defining and monitoring educational standards because their results are often used (in, for example, school performance tables) as output measures for accountability purposes. Public examination standards therefore underpin much of the public debate about educational standards generally and, indeed, are themselves the focus of controversy. To be able to engage critically with the public debate on standards, it is therefore necessary to understand the nature of examination standards and the extent to which, given their nature, they can legitimately be used to draw conclusions about educational standards. In this paper, I attempt to illuminate some of these issues.

Defining Public Examination Standards

The word *standards* is a notoriously slippery one. One of its more misleading aspects, when it is used in the context of educational assessment, is the image which it conjures up of standard measures in the physical sciences. Somewhere in France, we are told, there was once a bar of metal which defined the exact length of a metre. Where is the educational equivalent kept?

Proceedings of the British Academy, **102**, 69–120. © The British Academy 2000.

Once it is asked, the very strangeness of this question gives pause for thought. But what is actually wrong with the idea of a standard measure of educational attainment? Why can't we, for example, simply keep somewhere a copy of a Grade A GCSE script which, upon inspection, will enable us to see exactly what *GCSE Grade A* represents? The problem, of course, lies not in keeping the script but in being able to see what it represents. In practical terms, despite the deep philosophical waters surrounding primary and secondary properties or the possibility of objective knowledge, physical properties such as length are directly observable. Thus, when we look at an object exemplifying a length of 1 metre, we can directly observe its length and could use it to measure directly the length of a second physical object. To do this, we would simply hold the example alongside the second object and make a visual comparison.

With the general example of an examination script, however, we are dealing with a human linguistic artefact and to identify the standard which it represents we must interpret the language which it contains. This is a major difference from the case of physical properties. Interpretation of written text is far removed from direct observation and the meaning which a particular text has to an individual reader depends not only upon the text itself but also upon what the reader brings to it (see, for example, Eagleton 1993). Thus our standard script will represent something different, to a greater or lesser extent, to each reader. Moreover, an examination script does not encapsulate the whole of what it exemplifies. Educational attainments are complex networks of knowledge, skills and understandings, not all of which will be assessed on any one occasion nor, therefore, exemplified in any particular script. Thus, it is necessary to infer from the archive script what represents the same standard in the unrepresented aspects of the attainment being assessed. This has particular importance if we wish to compare the archive script with a second script. Not only will the second script require interpretation, but in general it will cover a somewhat different subset of the attainment being assessed. When the scripts are compared, the comparison cannot therefore be direct but must be a comparison of the two inferred standards, each of which is based upon an interpretation by the observer.

A popular response to this difference between physical and educational measurement is to try to construct explicit descriptions of educational standards and I shall look at this approach in more detail shortly. For the moment, however, we simply need to note that such descriptions are themselves linguistic artefacts and, in complex attainment domains, cannot be comprehensive. They therefore depend upon exactly similar processes of interpretation and inference to communicate standards as did our archive script. The upshot is that examination standards cannot be objective in the everyday sense in which standards relating to physical measurements are objective. The inevitable role of interpretation and inference in defining examination standards means that they are fundamentally subjective. That is to say, different observers will interpret the same student performance (or explicit description) differently, according to their different expectations and different notions of what constitutes attainment in the subject concerned.

To set an examination standard it is not therefore sufficient simply to identify a particular paradigmatic performance on a particular occasion, it is also necessary to address the question of how that performance should be interpreted and the implications which it has in terms of the wider range of attainments which make up the subject being examined. The detailed nature of *what* is measured by an examination is not obvious but a definition of it must be part of any useful definition of any particular examination standard.

In addition, the primary purpose of public examinations is to provide information for future meritocratic educational and vocational selection decisions (see Cresswell 1995 and 1997a, for detailed argument supporting this claim) and it is a feature of these selection processes that information from different examinations is combined and compared. As a result, it is essential, in terms of the notion of meritocratic fairness which underpins the use of examinations in selection, for all examinations of a particular family (e.g. GCSE) to report in terms of a common scale and for the same point on that scale to correspond to attainment with the same degree of merit for any examination in the family. That is, in examining jargon, the standards represented by the same grade from any examination in the family must be *comparable*. Other uses of examination results which treat grades from different examinations as interchangeable, such as school performance tables, also impose the same requirement.

Therefore, to define standards in a particular public examination in the way in which the term is normally understood, we must define:

1 what should be assessed;
2 the levels of attainment which are comparable to those represented by each grade in other examinations in the same family;

and to understand examination standards, we need to consider both of these aspects.

Turning, first, to the second aspect of examination standards, how can we determine whether the attainment required for the same grade is comparable in different examinations? To illustrate the difficulty of this question, take just a few specific examples: we require a Grade C in Mathematics to represent comparable attainment to a Grade C in Physics, a Grade C in English, a Grade C in French and a Grade C in Art. This requirement implies some way of making direct quantitative comparisons of candidates' attainments across disparate subjects. This is impossible because quantitative comparisons can only be made in terms of common features and the features which candidates' work in different subjects have in common are insufficiently relevant. That is to say, they refer to aspects of the work which are either irrelevant in terms of what should be assessed in one or both subjects (e.g. we could compare the physical properties, such as length, of candidates' answers but to what purpose?) or are only a part of what should be assessed in one or both subjects (e.g. quality of drawing, accuracy of spelling, arithmetic competence, and so on). To compare attainment in different subjects we are therefore left only with indirect bases for comparison, of which there are two: statistics and expert judgement, both of which I will look at in detail shortly.

First, however, we need briefly to consider the other aspect of examination standards: *what should be assessed?* Historically speaking, the curriculum in British schools evolved slowly, but continuously, to accommodate new approaches and developments. More recently, the curriculum has come under central control and short periods of comparative stability punctuated by imposed change may now be a more accurate description. In either case, however, the curriculum is not static and neither, therefore, is what is assessed in public examinations. The aspect of public examination standards which concerns what should be assessed therefore changes to reflect the current values of those in control of the curriculum or, where a national curriculum is not specified, those responsible for approving syllabuses. Moreover, it is not the case that such changes are necessarily small, as the following examples of changes in what is assessed illustrate: the introduction of 'modern' topics into mathematics syllabuses (and the accompanying removal of much Euclidean geometry) which began in the late 1960s, the removal during the 1970s, for ethical reasons, of dissection from

A-level Biology examinations; the change, for which the demands of international commerce were part of the public justification, to assessing communicative competence in modern foreign languages when GCSE was introduced in 1988; the continuous revision in what is assessed in examinations in computer studies to keep up with developing technology.

These examples illustrate the extent to which past examination standards have changed to reflect their evolving cultural context as well as overtly educational or pedagogical considerations. More subtle, but equally important, changes in what is assessed occur continuously in all school subjects, reflecting wider cultural changes in the way in which individual school subjects are perceived and contemporary expectations about students' achievements. Changes such as these, whether deliberate or evolutionary, mean that, as with the issue of comparability between subjects, the maintenance of comparable examination standards over time in what is nominally the same subject, actually requires quantitative comparisons to be made between qualitatively different attainments. Again, therefore, only indirect bases for comparison—statistics or expert judgement—can be used to maintain examination standards.[1] I will consider statistical approaches first.

Statistical Approaches

What is *comparable*, as applied to examination grade standards, normally taken to mean in statistical terms? In general, it is not taken to mean that an **individual** taking two comparable examinations should necessarily be awarded the same grade but is concerned, instead, with groups of candidates. For example, talking about the particular case of comparability between examining boards, the Forum on Comparability set up by the *Schools Council* (which had a general responsibility for British public examinations until the mid 1980s) said:

[1] In the evolutionary case, it is possible to argue that there is sufficient commonality between what will be assessed on any two adjacent occasions for practically useful, if slightly flawed, direct quantitative comparisons to be made between the attainments demonstrated by candidates. Even if this is exploited, however, there is an inherent *sorites* style paradox which means that, although standards are apparently maintained (within some close practical limit) between all adjacent years this does not guarantee their maintenance over long time periods. Most importantly, the accumulating qualitative changes in what is assessed and how it is evaluated force any check on the maintenance of standards over long periods to fall back on indirect means of comparison. I will return to this point later.

> ... the expectation is that had a group of examinees followed another board's syllabus and taken its examination, they might reasonably be expected to have obtained the same average grade.' (Schools Council 1979)

The definition of comparability implicit in this quotation can usefully be elaborated to cover the comparability of every grade, by replacing the reference to the 'average grade' by a reference to the **distribution** of grades for the group of candidates and in this paper I shall take *statistical comparability* to mean the identity of grade distributions. With this stance, a variety of different operational definitions of comparability are generated, depending upon the approach adopted to the problem of defining groups of candidates for which it is reasonable to expect identical grade distributions (see Cresswell 1996, for more details). However, my arguments below about the limitations of statistical definitions of comparable standards apply in general and do not depend crucially upon any particular definition.

Elsewhere (Cresswell 1996, 1997a, Goldstein and Cresswell 1996), I have set out in detail the conceptual problems surrounding statistical approaches to defining and maintaining comparable public examination standards in different examinations. Here, I will briefly summarise the two major ones. First, candidate attainment is affected by many variables, such as quality of teaching, student motivation and so on, as well as by examinations and their associated syllabuses. To illustrate the problem which follows from this, suppose that the standards in two examinations are set so as to produce identical grade distributions giving statistically defined comparability but that, subsequently, extensive guidance on effective teaching approaches for one of the syllabuses is provided. If this has the (presumably, desired) effect of improving the quality of teaching of the syllabus, the grade distributions of the two examinations will now differ and, according to our statistical definition, they will no longer set comparable standards *even if the question papers remain unchanged and are marked and graded identically.* This is not consistent with the way in which the notion of examination standards is normally interpreted and those who wish to use statistical definitions of comparable standards must either accept that they are open to continual revision[2] or argue that the standards originally set are to be

---

[2] This is, of course, catastrophic for those whose motive for using statistical approaches is a desire to make examination standards objective so that they can monitor changes in candidates' attainment over time. The continual revision of reference groups retains a sort of objectivity, but the price paid is the loss of any possibility of monitoring over time—the very reason for wanting objectivity in the first place. I shall return to this point later.

preferred, despite being based upon a comparison made on an arbitrary historical occasion.

The second major theoretical problem with statistical definitions of comparable standards concerns identifiable subgroups of candidates. Even when two grade distributions are identical for the whole groups of students whose attainment they describe, they need not be identical for well-defined subgroups within those groups. For example, the differences between boys' and girls' performances in GCSE examinations are well known and depend, at least in part, on the assessment techniques used (see, for example, Murphy 1982, Cresswell 1990) so that, if two examinations using different techniques have identical grade distributions for boys and girls combined, they will not necessarily have identical grade distributions for the boys and girls considered separately. Other reasons may produce similar disparities and GCSE English and Mathematics examinations illustrate the sorts of effects which occur in practice. Over the entire 16+ age cohort, the boys' grades in these two subjects are similarly distributed, but the girls' grade distributions differ substantially (Newton 1997a). It is unclear how this sort of effect can be accommodated if comparable standards are to be defined in terms of the identity of grade distributions. Are GCSE English and Mathematics standards comparable for boys but not for girls, *even though both boys' and girls' work is marked and graded identically?*[3] In the light of this, those wishing to define examination standards statistically have two choices again: re-define examination standards in a way which does not reflect their normal meaning (though it is not at all apparent, in this case, how this could be done) or defend the choice of an arbitrarily constituted group of candidates with which they define their standards.

In practice, even if the two theoretical problems discussed above are side-stepped by making arbitrary choices about the groups of candidates to be used and the occasions when comparable standards are to be defined in terms of the identity of grade distributions, major difficulties remain. Grade distributions reflect the attainments of the candidates who take the examinations and these attainments are the result of the interaction of many different variables. Systematic differences between the self-selected groups of candidates who take different examinations are therefore to be expected and so, in practice, it becomes necessary to attempt to control for such differences in the attainment of the candidates taking the different

---

[3] Ignoring any unintended gender bias which, in a recent study (Baird, 1998), was found not to be significant.

examinations before convincing statistically comparable standards can be established. Either an independent measure of attainment needs to be employed or indirect control of attainment can be attempted through school and student variables which influence it. Elsewhere (Cresswell 1996), I have reviewed in detail the various approaches of this type which have been tried in the past; here it is sufficient simply to note that the choice of relevant control variables inevitably involves value judgements and that different choices will lead to different operational definitions of comparable standards (for an example and an excellent discussion of the issues see Baird and Jones 1998).

The single most important lesson to draw from this discussion is that the use of statistical definitions of comparable standards does not, as is sometimes thought, lead to some sort of objectivity in examination standards. This is an illusion created by the technical layer which statistical approaches insert between the standards themselves and the, often implicit, value judgements which must underpin operational choices of historical baselines, specific reference groups of candidates and, in any practical system, appropriate control variables.

Judgemental Approaches

The other approach which can be used to set examination standards is to use expert judgement to define the levels of performance in a particular examination which represent standards comparable to those represented by the grades awarded via other examinations in the same family. This approach is theoretically coherent, provided that the judgements involved are accepted as *value* judgements, because, as most philosophers of value argue, value judgements do not ascribe properties to the objects being judged.[4] As a result, setting standards via judgements of the relative value of candidates' attainments in different subjects does not involve making quantitative comparisons between qualitatively differing attainments. Thus, using expert judgement to define examination standards is theoretically justified, provided that the judges are seen as expressing their subjective view about the value of the candidates' attainments and not as identifying some objective property of the attainments which, by virtue of their expertise, they can recognise.

---

[4] For general discussion on this point from a range of philosophical perspectives see, for example, Ayer (1946), Fogelin (1967), and Billington (1988). French *et al.* (1987) argued the same case specifically for judgements of educational attainment.

Moreover, the judgemental approach to defining examination standards is not vulnerable to the same theoretical problems as the use of statistical definitions since it does not make the standards depend directly upon the performance of candidates. Thus, for example, changing differences between the proportions of boys and girls who meet a judgementally determined standard have no implications for the coherence of the standard itself, nor does an internal inconsistency arise if the outcomes in one examination change relative to another. In theory, such changes can be interpreted directly as changes in the attainment of the candidates, as valued by the judges.

Of course, to argue that setting examination standards is not a matter of identifying performances which meet some set of objective criteria but is a process of subjective judgement more akin to evaluating a work of art or literature, raises immediate questions about its acceptability. Value judgements are usually seen as subjective and irrational as a consequence of the affective component which they contain (as in: *I don't know much about Art, but I know what I like*). However, this says more about our everyday notions of expertise and rationality than it says about value judgements. It has long been recognised that, although value judgements cannot be facts amenable to empirical verification or epistemological justification, they can, nonetheless, be the results of a rational process and be supported by reasons (Fogelin 1967, Beardsley 1981) if not pure deductive or inductive reasoning (Best 1985). Moreover, there is now considerable neurological evidence to suggest that feeling is an essential, if unrecognised, part of what we would normally class as rational thought (Damasio 1995) so that deductive or inductive reasoning is rarely, if ever, the sole basis for the decisions which human beings make. Value judgements are no different. Although they are subjective, they can be based upon reasoned argument, are not necessarily simply emotional or intuitive responses and should not, therefore, be assumed to be irrational, necessarily capricious or, indeed, unreliable (in the sense of being difficult to replicate). In fact, ten years ago, Frances Good and I obtained levels of agreement equivalent to marking reliabilities above 0.95 between different groups of examiners judging the quality of GCSE scripts in History, French and Physics (Good and Cresswell 1988a).

However, the reliability and rationality of value judgements is not always easily accepted and, in Britain in the last 15 years or so, there have been many attempts to create more objective judgemental systems for setting examination standards via systems of explicit criteria and aggregation rules. If, as I have just argued, setting examination standards is an evaluative process, it seems reasonable at first sight, as Christie and Forrest (1981) proposed, to try to identify the criteria which judges use, and how they use them, when they decide the relative merits of candidates' work and thus the grades which they should be awarded. I call this approach *strong criterion-referencing* and give an extensive discussion of the ways in which it differs from more conventional criterion-referencing in Cresswell (1997a). Implicit within it is an over-simplified model of the process of human judgement which has considerable intuitive appeal.

This implicit model sees the process of setting standards as one which involves judging the relative merits of students' work (for example, their examination scripts) by using a fixed set of *criteria* which epitomise work of varying standards in each of a number of different *dimensions* of attainment. In conventional practice, the criteria are *tacit*, in that they exist only in judges' heads, but strong criterion-referencing assumes them to be capable of explicit expression, given sufficient introspection and linguistic ingenuity. Having decided the relative quality of the work in terms of each dimension of attainment, the judge is then thought to synthesise an overall judgement of each script as a whole by combining the judgements on the separate dimensions using a process of rational thought. It is assumed in strong criterion-referencing that there are implicit high level computational procedures which produce this synthesis and, again, that these procedures are capable of being made explicit, given sufficient introspection. This view of judgement is thus an essentially mechanical and dualist one, in which the judges first formulate a description of each candidate's work in terms of criteria on several different dimensions and then consider their description, presumably in some sort of *Cartesian theatre* (Dennett 1993) in their heads, so that they can apply high level computational rules to determine its overall value.

I call this view of judgement the *Cartesian Computer Model* and it might help to make it clearer if I outline how it was operationalised in one recent attempt to make it concrete: the approach initially used in England and Wales for National Curriculum Assessment at the end of Key Stage 3. Here, the different *Attainment Targets* of National Curriculum subjects represented the different dimensions, each consisting of 10 levels of increasing competence (since reduced to 8) defined by 10 sets of explicit criteria called *Statements of Attainment* (now re-written in whole sentences and called *Level Descriptions*). Candidates were assigned to a level on each Attainment Target separately and then explicit aggregation rules were used to produce a single overall level for each candidate from his or her separate levels on the Attainment Targets.

Readers who doubt the intuitive appeal of the Cartesian Computer Model, and suspect me of erecting a straw man, should reflect upon its remarkable tenacity, in association with the strong criterion-referencing meme, in the face of repeated failure. In the 1980s, there was a considerable amount of work done in Britain on the notion of *grade criteria* for public examinations (Hadfield, 1980 [quoted in Christie and Forrest, 1981]; Orr and Nuttall, 1983; SEC, 1984; Forrest and Orr, 1984; Orr and Forrest, 1984; Bardell *et al* 1984; SEC 1985; Long, 1985; SEC, 1986; SEC,1987). This work assumed the Cartesian Computer model, being based on the view that standards can be encapsulated in written criteria which prescribe the level of attainment required to justify the award of a particular grade. However, although it was possible to write standard-setting grade criteria (either *ab initio* as in the original SEC work or as a result of perusing candidates' scripts, as in later work), in use they proved not to apply to some candidates' performances which were awarded the grades in question by conventional procedures. Gerry Forrest and his colleagues (Forrest and Orr 1984; Orr and Forrest 1984, Bardell *et al*. 1984), in their general conclusions, published in the reports of all their studies, observed:

> performances in existing examinations that would result in the award of particular grades may not qualify for those grades if the criteria considered relevant were applied.

Since then, further attempts to make the Cartesian Computer model of judgement operational, most notably the early National Curriculum assessments, have also failed. The most recent failure is visible in the apparently endless process of revision of the assessment models used for General National Vocational Qualifications and Key Skills. In fact, no strongly criterion-referenced public assessment system has ever been made to work successfully, given that success means replacing holistic value judgements of quality with an equivalent set of explicit criteria and aggregation rules. It is, of course, possible to challenge this definition of success but the consequence of using explicit criteria and aggregation rules which are not successful in these terms is that the examinations concerned do not meet commonly accepted requirements related to fairness (see Cresswell 1987, Cresswell and Houston 1991, Cresswell 1994 and Cresswell 1997b for more on this aspect). In any case, the intention of work on public examination grade criteria has always been to make the standards represented by the existing holistically judged grades explicit, not to change them.

A fundamental problem with grading systems based upon explicit criteria and aggregation rules is that they view the task of judges as involving the identification of a set of observable well-defined qualities in candidates' work. In fact, as Sadler (1987) has argued, the criteria which are appropriate for any particular educational value judgement differ according to the nature of the work being evaluated. This has long been recognised as a feature of judgements of value in other fields (see, for example, Aldrich 1963). Indeed, the presence of the same quality may be reason to value one object highly but not another, because other features of the second object change the value attached to the quality in question (Pole 1961). Modern students of literary criticism also argue that the nature of the work modifies the criteria relevant to its evaluation (Eagleton 1993). Moreover, work on the psychology of evaluative judgement is consistent with these views. Eiser (1990) reviews the relevant empirical psychological evidence, and shows that it strongly suggests that a person presented with new information searches for relevant conceptual categories with which to encode it, starting with those immediately accessible in memory and continuing until sufficient (according to some internal criterion) relevant ones are found. In addition, the 30 year-long failure of rule-based artificial intelligence to reproduce human expertise outside very tightly systematised domains is now beginning to be seen as evidence that human expertise does not involve the rapid application of very complex high-level rules. Authors such as Dreyfus (1992) and Devlin (1997) argue that what distinguishes an expert is precisely that he or she has transcended such rules and developed holistic skills specific to his or her area of expertise.[5]

---

[5] Although it may be possible to reproduce expert behaviour in some domains using systems of catalogued knowledge and high-level rules, the formation of evaluative judgements of educational attainment looks unlikely to be such a domain. Such judgements require the implicit formation of statements like 'This script has enough of the properties required for a Grade A.' According to Copeland (1993) the set of valid sentences of this type is formally *undecidable*—that is to say, there is no algorithmic process which can always determine if a sentence is a member of this set—it follows that no computational rule, however complex it is, can be guaranteed to produce the correct overall evaluation from all possible quantitative judgements on various dimensions unless the set of those quantitative judgements is finite, which seems unlikely. It is also worth noting that recent practical attempts to use Artificial Intelligence-style techniques to categorise students' answers to free-response test questions use a brute force statistical modelling approach which the researchers concerned (Burstein *et al.* 1997) suggest is best used *alongside* but not *in place of* human judgement.

Thus, the human evaluative process does not involve the application of a limited and well-defined set of criteria which have been determined beforehand to be relevant to all objects of a particular class, and nor is it exhaustive or rule-based. The above mutually supporting philosophical arguments and empirical evidence reveal the fundamental reason why strong criterion-referencing, involving the application of explicit written criteria according to the Cartesian Computer Model of judgement, does not, and cannot, replicate value judgements made by suitably qualified judges.[6]

A more suitable model for the process used by examiners evaluating students' examination work is the *Multiple Zen Drafts Model*. This model of judgement sees the judges as engaged in a constant process of evaluation and re-evaluation as they read the candidate's work. There is no need for a pre-existing set of evaluative criteria and therefore no set of computational rules for reaching an overall judgement. However, there is normally reasonable agreement between different judges about which features of candidates' work are likely to be relevant to its evaluation. The evaluation is direct and immediate in the somewhat metaphysical way celebrated by Pirsig (1974) in *Zen and the Art of Motorcycle Maintenance* but is continuously open to revision (redrafting—hence *multiple drafts*) as the judge reads more of the work. The judge reads and re-reads the work until his or her evaluation stabilises. (See Dennett 1993 for an extensive discussion of *multiple drafts* as a model of consciousness in general).

The Multiple Zen Drafts Model is consistent with modern understandings of the nature of critical evaluation, particularly with *Reader Response (or Reception) Theory*. I can do no better to explain Multiple Zen Drafts further than quote part of Eagleton's (1993) description of the process of reading:

> . . . the reader will bring to the work certain 'pre-understandings', a dim context of beliefs and expectations within which the work's various features will be assessed. As the reading process proceeds, however, these expectations

---

[6] This is not, however, to say that concise statements cannot be constructed which, in Wilmut and Rose's (1989) terms, 'convey the flavour' of a grade. Such *grade descriptions* have been included in GCSE syllabuses, for example, since 1988 and describe a paradigmatic attainment worthy of the grade, rather than the attainment of every candidate awarded the grade. Although, for the reasons given, grade descriptions cannot be used as criteria for objectively judging the attainment of all candidates, they can form a useful focus for building consensus among examiners about the sorts of qualities attached to scripts which they judge worthy of a particular grade and can thereby help to facilitate agreement between different examiners' qualitative judgements.

will themselves be modified by what we learn, and the hermeneutical circle—
moving from part to whole and back to part—will begin to revolve. . . . What
we have learnt on page one will fade and become 'foreshortened' in memory,
perhaps to be radically qualified by what we learn later. Reading is not a
straightforward linear movement, a merely cumulative affair: our initial
speculations generate a frame of reference within which to interpret what
comes next, but what comes next may retrospectively transform our original
understanding . . .

(Eagleton 1993: 77)

There is a certain irony in the fact that Reader Response Theory, as
such, was developing during the 1970s and early 1980s, at the very time
when educational assessment was most obsessed with the essentially
mechanical Cartesian Computer Model of evaluation enshrined in the
notion of criterion-referencing and the associated attempts to render
evaluative criteria completely explicit. Few public examination awarders
would fail to recognise the similarity between the process described by
Eagleton and their own experience of judging candidates' scripts.

The Nature of Examination Standards

The preceding analysis leads to only one conclusion: examination standards are not, *and cannot be made*, objective[7]—they are social constructs.
The need for all definitions of examination standards to define *what* must
be assessed requires judgements of a non-technical nature to be made,
relating to issues such as the wider social value of different educational
attainments. Less obviously, even within a single school subject, what is to
be assessed and the perceived value of particular levels of attainment
change over time to reflect contemporary concerns so that standards
only have meaning within their own social context, localised in time
and space.[8] As a result the bases upon which candidates separated in
time can be assessed are different, making direct quantitative comparisons of their performance invalid (see also Goldstein 1983 and Cresswell
1997a). Only indirect statistical comparisons or qualitative value judgements can provide a theoretically valid basis for the comparison of
performances from different occasions in domains which change over

[7] This is not to say that the assessments of individual examination candidates cannot be
'objective' in the sense of being free of significant biases and reliable; indeed, recent research
on these matters is reasonably reassuring (see Baird 1998 and Newton 1996).
[8] Interested readers can consult Cresswell (1996 and 1997a) or Wiliam (1996a and 1996b) for
more detailed discussion of the socially constructed nature of examination standards and its
implications.

time and both of these approaches involve subjectivity, whether in the process of judging candidates' work or in the arbitrary choice of statistical reference groups. It follows that the objective measurement of quantitative changes in educational standards is impossible.

However, these are theoretical concerns and a tough-minded pragmatist might well argue that they are somewhat precious. Such a critic needs to know why, if subjectivity is simply acknowledged as inevitable, public examination results cannot still be used as one fallible quantitative measure of changes in educational standards in the same way as the retail prices index, the composition of which also varies over time, is used as one measure of domestic inflation. After all, he or she might argue, the examination boards claim to maintain the same standard from one year to the next, albeit by the use of qualitative judgement and/or statistics based upon reasonable but arbitrary decisions. Surely, therefore, comparisons of the statistics of examination outcomes over long periods of time must tell us something about changing overall standards of attainment. To respond to this challenge, in the next section I take a practical look at the processes by which comparable public examination standards are maintained from year to year and draw out the implications of those processes for the interpretation of changes in examination statistics over time.

Maintaining Examination Standards in Practice

In the British public examination system a new examination is set each year on any particular syllabus and there is therefore a need to establish a new pass mark for each grade (these marks are called the *grade boundaries* in examining parlance) on each successive version of the examination. Grade boundaries cannot simply be carried forward unchanged from one examination to the next because the papers inevitably vary somewhat in difficulty from year to year, requiring compensating changes in the marks required for the award of each grade if the standards of attainment demanded for those grades are to be comparable between years. To determine the new positions of the grade boundaries, awarding meetings are held in which senior examiners make judgements about the quality of work of sample candidates' scripts and combine the qualitative data produced by this process with statistical evidence to arrive at final recommendations for the positions of the grade boundaries. The process is specified in outline in QCA (1998) and described in detail in Cresswell (1997a). Its use of qualitative judgement and indirect statistical evidence is consistent with the theoretical analysis I gave in the preceding sections. Although, in practice, both qualitative judgement and statistical data are used to maintain examination standards, it is instructive to consider these two sources of evidence separately.

Using Expert Qualitative Judgement

Turning to qualitative judgement first, how effective is it for maintaining examination standards? That is to say, can examiners, by scrutinising candidates' answers to examination papers, identify the mark which corresponds to the same standard of attainment as a given grade boundary mark in the preceding version of the examination? If they can, then any changes in the examination outcomes which follow from their qualitative judgements will arise from changes in the attainment of the candidates between years, not from any differences in difficulty which there may be between the two years' examinations. On the other hand, differences in outcome which could be shown to be related to the examination itself would imply that the judgemental process had failed to take into account those differences in difficulty. Thus, considering changes in the examination outcomes which would follow from only the judgemental part of the awarding process, casts light on the adequacy of qualitative judgement *per se* as a method of maintaining standards. The question is: can the scale and nature of such changes in outcomes reasonably be explained only by changes in the attainment of the candidates or is there reason to believe that effects due to the examination and its awarding are also present? This section addresses this question.

However, it is essential to be clear about the nature of the investigations which I report here. In the absence of independent information about the attainments of the candidates, it is impossible to disentangle the effects of candidate attainment and examination difficulty within any observed changes in a *particular* examination's statistics. This section therefore considers the balance of probabilities, based upon an investigation of many different examinations. This essentially statistical approach enables the existence to be demonstrated, with a high level of probability, of changes in examination outcomes which are due to the examinations, rather than the candidates. It does *not*, however, enable the particular examinations in which such effects operated to be identified.

Table 1 shows the changes produced between two successive examination occasions in the cumulative percentages of candidates

Table 1. Comparisons between the outcomes in two successive examinations derived from purely judgemental data for a sample of A−level examinations with more than 500 candidates.

Subject	Number of candidates in		Change in cumulative percentage at		
	Year 1	Year 2	Grade A	Grade B	Grade E
Accounting	6775	6637	−1.4	−3.9	−0.1
Applied Mathematics	1359	1237	−6.5	−3.4	0.1
Biology I	4152	5159	−4.2	−9.4	−12.4
Biology II	2195	2464	−5.0	−8.4	−12.7
Business Studies	11206	12477	1.3	3.2	6.2
Chemistry	3902	4139	−2.7	−5.8	−8.0
Communication Studies	3945	4565	2.5	6.4	2.1
Computing	3445	3294	−2.6	−4.2	−0.7
Constitutional Law	701	669	0.0	0.8	13.6
Economic & Social History	928	1066	−1.2	−2.6	−4.4
Economics	12056	11913	0.1	−0.8	−0.9
English I (Language & Literature)	11196	12186	−0.3	−2.1	−0.9
English II (Literature)	4401	3680	−4.8	−11.4	0.1
English III (Literature Alternative)	10061	13929	4.2	0.9	−3.6
Environmental Science	562	794	−0.2	0.4	1.4
French	4492	5324	1.2	5.4	5.1
General Studies	1141	1256	2.8	6.6	8.9
Geography	2813	3026	1.4	8.8	9.0
German	1706	2140	−1.6	−7.0	−10.0
Government & Politics	1658	1835	0.1	−2.9	1.8
History	5234	5894	0.0	−2.2	−4.2
History (Alternative)	2125	2397	−0.6	−1.6	−3.4
History of Art	1233	1226	1.9	8.5	6.0
Human Biology	2832	3300	0.0	0.1	0.4
Law	3747	4166	−4.2	−3.8	−0.1
Philosophy	476	699	−3.8	−4.1	−15.3
Photography	1335	1307	0.9	0.4	0.0
Physics	7412	7423	0.0	−2.8	−5.2
Physical Education	222	630	0.4	1.6	−1.1
Psychology	8504	10120	1.1	1.2	4.0
Pure & Applied Mathematics	6718	6647	−0.3	0.6	−0.2
Pure Mathematics	3219	3137	−13.2	−15.7	−4.4
Pure Mathematics & Statistics	5464	5432	0.4	1.6	−1.4
Sociology	19789	17222	0.5	−2.7	0.7
Spanish	773	928	−4.0	−11.8	−10.7
Sport Studies	477	749	−0.3	−1.8	2.4
Statistics	1939	1778	2.0	9.8	9.9
Theatre Studies	4749	5634	−0.9	−0.5	−1.4

awarded each of three grades, when the grade boundaries were fixed purely by a process of qualitative judgement of candidates' work. The data relate to grades A, B and E in a broad range of A-Level examinations which attracted over 500 candidates in the year in which the data were collected. Some examinations exhibit small changes in overall outcomes between the two years, some examinations exhibit large ones. One point immediately worth making is that there is no obvious relationship between the nature of the subjects and the scale of the changes.

In public examination awarding procedures, examiners are asked to explain any large changes in the proportions of candidates who would be awarded each grade as a result of their qualitative judgements. Three possible explanations, one or more of which will be offered by the awarders in any particular subject, are usually proposed. In *Explanation Number 1*, the examiners simply argue that the entire group of candidates, as such, are better (or worse) than the previous year's group. In *Explanation Number 2* they go a little deeper and refer to any changes there may have been in the relative proportions of candidates entered by different types of centres or in the gender balance within the entry. (Descriptive information about the composition of the entry is routinely available to awarding meetings in terms of these two variables.) *Explanation Number 3* concerns the case where the number of candidates entering for the examination has changed considerably. It may then be suggested by the examiners that the candidates who have been gained or lost, as a group, are better (or worse) than the rest of the candidates.

In the following sections, I examine each of the examiners' three explanations, in the context of the data as shown in Table 1.

Explanation Number 1: As a whole, the candidates as a group are simply better (or worse)
By itself, this is not an explanation at all for a change in the proportions of candidates in each grade, it is simply a restatement of the implications of the grade boundary judgements in a different form. Since it is offered by the same individuals who have made the judgements which it purports to explain, it is not independent corroboration of the results of those judgements and cannot, logically, explain them.

However, this explanation is interesting because of the implied models which are held by those who proffer it. The explanation could be based upon the notion that systematic overall attainment changes are to be expected because of changing educational policy and practice or other external factors; or it could be the reflection of an implicit assumption that some variation is to be expected between the results of adjacent years' candidates simply because they are different groups of students; or it could be referring to both of these potential causes for variations in examination outcomes. I will consider the second cause first. Given that it is clearly a possibility, the obvious question to ask is: how large are the random variations which can be expected in the statistics of public examination results? This question effectively views each year's candidates for a particular examination as a sample from the population of all candidates who take that examination over its lifetime. Posed like this, it is essentially a question for sampling theory.

If a few plausible assumptions are made about the nature of examination candidate populations and the randomness of any particular year's entry (see Cresswell 1997a), then it is straightforward to evaluate the size of the differences in examination results statistics which might be expected as a result of chance differences between successive years' entries. The standard test for the significance of differences between proportions in large samples can be used to evaluate the statistic, z, which is theoretically normally distributed with a mean of 0 and variance of 1. If this test is applied to the data producing Table 1 (see Cresswell 1997a, for details), the results summarised in Figure 1 are obtained. Clearly, the differences in outcomes between the two years cannot reasonably be viewed as the results of random variations between successive groups of candidates.

It follows that some effect other than straightforward sampling error is operating in many of the cases in Table 1. It might be argued that the prior ability or motivation of the groups of candidates entered for the different examinations changed significantly between Years 1 and 2 for some systematic reasons. Possible causes of such a change might include, for example, widespread medical factors or social ones such as growing fear of unemployment, although such extrinsic factors seem unlikely to affect different school subjects differentially, as they would have to do to explain the data in Figure 1. Alternatively, in the terms of Explanation Number 1, the causes of the changes in outcomes between the two years must be improvement or deterioration in the quality of educational provision in the subjects concerned. Thus, to evaluate Explanation Number 1, the key question is whether changes in the overall ability or motivation of candidates or in educational provision could be the causes of the significant changes in examination outcome illustrated as shown in Figure 1.

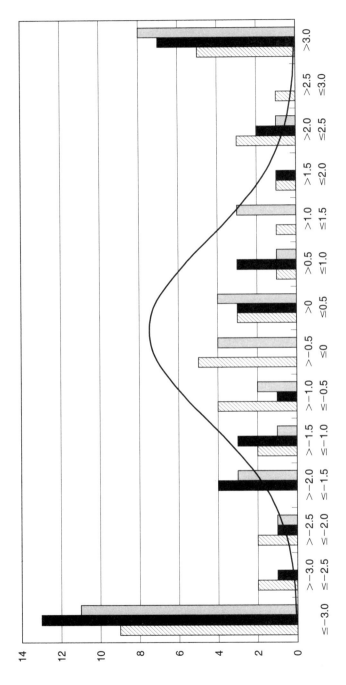

Figure 1. Distribution of *z* statistics for differences between judgemental outcomes in two years for a sample of A-level examinations. (▢) A, (■) B, (▢) E, (——) normal.

With the data available, this question cannot be unequivocally answered. However, evidence relevant to it can be obtained by considering the changes in outcomes which would follow from the judgements for subgroups of candidates whose origins are different and whose educational provision is differently organised. This has been done for the examinations in Table 1 by looking separately at the changes in outcomes between Years 1 and 2 for UK candidates from schools, UK candidates from further education colleges and overseas candidates (the detailed data are contained in Cresswell 1997a). In all, there are 67 cases in Table 1 where there is a significant difference between Years 1 and 2 in the cumulative proportion of all candidates at a key grade boundary. In 47 of these cases, a change in the same direction occurs for all three subgroups of candidates and, in the remaining 20 cases, such a change occurs for 2 out of the three subgroups.

Moreover, if the same analysis is done for the changes in outcomes in the same subjects between Year 1 and the preceding year (the full data are, again, given in Cresswell 1997a) and the results are compared with those illustrated in Figure 1, it is clear that the annual changes in outcome between these adjacent pairs of years are little related to each other—see Figure 2. It is difficult to identify any plausible extrinsic factors or educational mechanisms which could not only differentially affect overall attainment in different subjects on a global scale so markedly, but also produce effects which vary so much from one year's

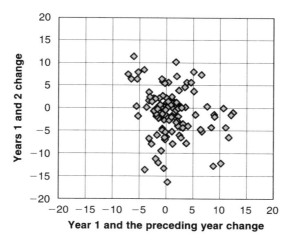

Figure 2. Relationship between z statistics of changes in outcomes for Year 1 and the preceding year versus Years 1 and 2.

cohort of candidates to another. On balance, therefore, Explanation Number 1 appears insufficient to explain the scale of changes observed, between years 1 and 2, in the proportions of candidates awarded each grade if qualitative judgements of candidates' work *are the only data* used to maintain standards. Any mechanism capable of generating the changes observed would have to operate through something which all subgroups of candidates within an annual cohort have in common but which changes annually. The examination itself is the only known factor which meets these requirements.

Explanation Number 2: The balance of centre types and/or genders has changed

This explanation seems at first sight to be a plausible one. Clearly, if there are differences in attainment between different subgroups of candidates, then variations in the relative proportions of these subgroups will lead to changes in the overall proportions of candidates awarded each grade. Is this effect sufficient to explain the differences observed in Table 1?

To explore this question, the grade distributions for subgroups of candidates in Year 1 (see Cresswell 1997a) were combined, re-weighted in such a way as to reflect the relative proportions of each subgroup in Year 2, as follows:

$$P'_x = \sum_j P_{jx} \cdot s'_j$$

where P'_x is the predicted proportion of Year 2 candidates exceeding the boundary for Grade x,

P_{jx} is the proportion of Year 1 candidates in Subgroup j exceeding the boundary for Grade x

and s'_j is the proportion of candidates in Subgroup j in Year 2

The changes in outcome predicted in this way were then compared with the actual changes in overall grade distribution between the two years. Clearly, any differences between the actual changes in outcomes and the ones predicted by re-weighting indicate discrepancies which cannot be accounted for by changes in the composition of the entry between the two years, at least with respect to the subgroups referred to in Explanation Number 2. The observed differences are not only very much larger than those predicted but also uncorrelated with them (see Cresswell 1997a, for the detailed analysis and a demonstration that, in general, realistic changes in subgroup distributions are unlikely to produce large changes in overall examination outcomes). Explanation Number 2 is not, therefore sufficient to account, in general, for the scale of changes observed in the outcomes of successive years' examinations if qualitative judgement *alone* is used in an attempt to maintain grade standards.

Explanation Number 3: This year's new (missing) candidates are better (or worse) than the rest

This explanation, which is sometimes offered by examiners when the number of candidates entering for an examination has grown or shrunk considerably, is essentially a special case of Explanation Number 2 in which the new (or missing) candidates are thought of as a subgroup of candidates with zero incidence in the previous (or current) year. As a result, the plausibility of Explanation Number 3 as a sufficient explanation for observed changes in grade outcomes is similar to that of Explanation Number 2. Only if the entry for an examination grows or shrinks substantially as a result of many different centres making similar changes to their entry policies and entering candidates from a different range of attainment, can Explanation Number 3 account for large changes in the proportions of candidates awarded each grade. However, as Table 1 exemplifies, year-on-year changes in the number of candidates entering for an examination are rarely large in proportion to the existing entry.

The relationship between examiners' judgements and the statistics of the candidates' marks

It appears very probable, therefore, that the differences in outcomes reported in Table 1 are due, at least in part, to fluctuations in the standards represented by the examiners' qualitative judgements. As was noted earlier, it is not possible, in the absence of independent assessments of the candidates' achievements, to *prove* this conclusion in any *particular* case, nor to estimate the precise size of the discrepancies which occur. However, it is possible to establish upper bound estimates for the movements in grade boundaries[9] which would have been required to set standards in Year 2 which were comparable to those in Year 1. If it is assumed that the attainments of the Year 2 candidates were distributed identically to those of the Year 1 candidates, then changes in the distributions of marks between the two years

---

[9] By convention, the *grade boundary* is the lowest mark on the examination awarded to work which merits the grade in question.

can be interpreted as indicating changes in the difficulty of the question papers and/or changes in the severity of the marking process. Since the purpose of awarding comparable standards is to make adjustments to grade boundaries which compensate for such changes, estimates of the positions of the Year 2 grade boundaries can then be obtained by scaling the grade boundaries used in Year 1 in accordance with the means and standard deviations of the Years 1 and 2 mark scales, as follows:

$$B'_x = \frac{(B_x - m_y)}{s_y} \cdot s_{y+1} + m_{y+1}$$

where B'_x is the new position of the boundary B_x for Grade x

$\quad\quad m_y$ is the mean score in year y

and $\quad s_y$ is the standard deviation of scores in year y

The results of doing this have been compared with the positions of the grade boundaries based solely upon examiner judgement in Year 2, producing Figure 3 which plots the actual movements of the grade boundaries against the movements predicted on the basis of the changes in the mark statistics. (Two of the examinations in Table 1 have been excluded because their maximum mark changed substantially between Years 1 and 2, producing misleadingly extreme movements.) It can be seen that there is a fairly strong relationship between the predicted and actual grade boundary movements but that, on average, the size of the actual movements is about 0.4 of the size of the predicted ones. From this analysis, it appears that the examiners correctly identified the direction of the changes required but, given the present assumption that the candidates were of comparable achievement in the two years, failed to take sufficient account of the change in difficulty of the examination papers and/or their marking.

Although the assumption upon which the present analysis is based is exactly that, an assumption, it is important to note that, in 81 (77 per cent) of cases, the qualitative judgements moved the boundaries in the *direction* implied by the mark statistics, if not to the *extent*. Thus, in these cases, the judgements confirm that, to some extent at least, the mark statistics reflect changes in the difficulty of the examinations. However, there is no reason to believe that any change there might be in the attainment of the candidates from one year to the next is not independent of any change in the difficulty of the examination which occurs. Therefore, if the reasonable assumption is made that the candi-

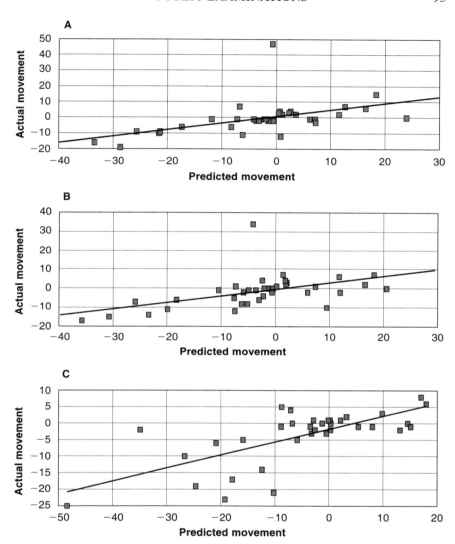

Figure 3. Actual movement of Grade boundaries in Year 2, against movement predicted from change in mark statistics.

A.	Grade A boundary	$y = 0.4156x + 0.6181$	$R^2 = 0.2504$
B.	Grade B boundary	$y = 0.3407x - 0.5835$	$R^2 = 0.2545$
E.	Grade E boundary	$y = 0.3928x - 1.7727$	$R^2 = 0.4898$

dates are equally likely to be slightly better or slightly worse from one year to the next, the actual movement of the grade boundaries should be less than that predicted from the change in mark statistics in 50 per cent of cases and greater than the predicted change in the remaining 50 per cent. However, of the 81 cases where the mark statistics and judges agree on the direction of the move, the actual move is less than the predicted move in 57. Using the binomial distribution, the two-tailed probability of this (or a more extreme value) occurring by chance is easily shown to be less than 0.001. This strongly suggests that, for some of these examinations at least, the examiners' qualitative judgements took insufficient account of changes in the difficulty of the examination papers and/or their marking.

This conclusion is entirely consistent with Frances Good and my (Good and Cresswell 1988a and 1988b) earlier experimental result that judges tend towards relative severity when setting grade boundaries on harder papers within tiered examinations. It seems reasonable to conclude that qualitative judgement alone is inadequate as a method of maintaining examination grade standards from year to year because it does not take sufficient account of changes in the difficulty of successive year's examinations. Some of the reasons for this relate to psychological and sociological aspects of the judgemental process which have recently been studied in detail (see Murphy *et al.* 1996, and Cresswell 1997a). Earlier, I set out at some length the reasons why attempts to reduce the process of qualitative judgement to a more mechanical activity involving explicit criteria and rules for reaching overall judgements based upon them—what I call strong criterion-referencing—does not offer a solution to this problem and has failed every time it has been attempted. The only alternative method of maintaining examination standards is therefore the use of statistical evidence either instead of, or alongside, qualitative judgement.

Using Statistics

There are several different statistical approaches, of varying technical sophistication, which could be used, by themselves, as the basis for maintaining examination standards from year to year (see Cresswell 1996 for a review). In practice, however, the procedures which the examining boards' use combine statistical data with qualitative judgement, as required by the regulator's *Code of Practice* (QCA 1998). In essence, the statistical parts of the procedures assume that large changes in outcomes from one year to the next are implausible for examinations with reasonably large entries from a stable group of schools. Analyses of the results in the previous and current year of only those centres which enter candidates in both years are sometimes used when there are reasons to doubt this assumption but the use of these analyses does not change the argument in this section. Similarly, analyses which consider the effects of changes in the types of centres entering candidates or which use considerations of value-added or any other of the approaches which I reviewed in Cresswell (1996) may be used but, again, without changing the essential argument. In the interests of clarity, I shall therefore refer throughout this section only to the conventional approach in which similar statistical outcomes are expected from year to year for any particular examination.

In normal British examining practice, the combination of statistical and judgemental data is, itself, a judgemental process (QCA 1998). Formal methods such as, for example, the use of Bayes' theorem are not used (see Cresswell 1997a for further discussion). However, there is no doubt that the statistical data have a significant influence on the examination standards which are set and, thus, on the overall examination outcomes. Figures 4 and 5 show the equivalent data to Figures 1 and 3 when current awarding procedures, combining judgement and statistical data are used (see Cresswell 1997a, for more detail).

Figure 4 brings us to the crux of the issue over the maintenance of examination standards and the use of examination results to monitor educational standards. Is the slight upward movement in the outcomes the result of improved attainment in some examinations or of a slight tendency to leniency in the statistically informed standard-setting process? Or, more realistically, perhaps we should ask: to what *extent* is the slight upward movement in the outcomes due to improved attainment and to what *extent* is it due to the awarding process itself? Unfortunately but inevitably, there are no data available from the examinations themselves which enable this question to be answered.

What is clear, is that the active use, during the annual process of setting examination standards, of assumptions of statistical continuity between examination results in successive years means that the statistics of examination outcomes do not necessarily reflect changes in the attainment of candidates which occur over time. The very process of awarding removes, to some unknown extent, the effects of any such changes from the examination statistics. This makes it, at the least, potentially misleading to try to use public examination results for the long term monitoring of educational standards. Unfortunately, as the data reported earlier showed, if assumptions of statistical continuity are not made, the alternative unsupported qualitative judgements of students' work are insufficiently stable for their results to be interpreted

Mike Cresswell

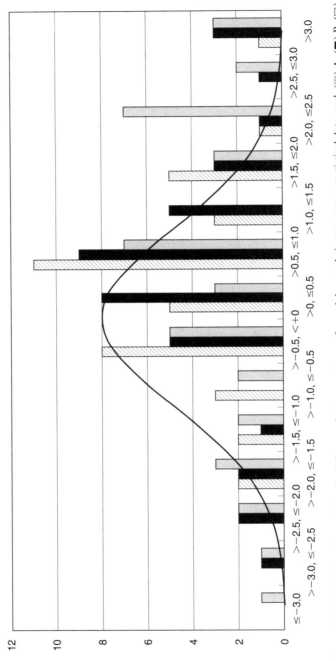

Figure 4. Distribution of z statistics for differences between outcomes for each key grade in two years—statistical data used. (▨) A, (■) B, (□) E, (——) normal.

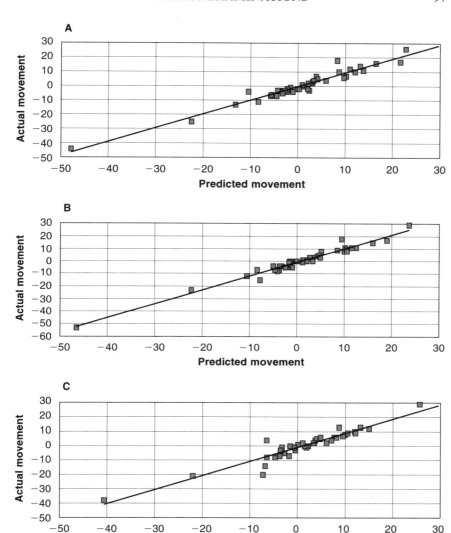

Figure 5. Actual movement of Grade boundaries in Year 2, against movement predicted from change in mark statistics—statistical data used.

A. Grade A boundary $y = 0.9643x - 0.3875$ $R^2 = 0.9423$
B. Grade B boundary $y = 1.1048x - 0.9194$ $R^2 = 0.9629$
E. Grade E boundary $y = 0.9822x - 0.9577$ $R^2 = 0.8966$

as reliable indicators of changing standards of attainment among examination candidates.

Moreover, the problem would not be solved (though it might be illuminated) by measures such as pre-testing public examination questions. The very high-stakes nature of public examinations for the candidates themselves means that problems of motivation and preparedness afflict non-operational pre-tests and, in any case, the need for security of the examinations means that papers could not be pre-tested in their entirety. Here, in conditions which reflect the historic purpose of public examinations—to award qualifications—lie some of the practical reasons why it is problematic to interpret the data which they produce in terms of changes in educational standards over time.

Similarly, the use of statistically informed qualitative judgement to set annual standards is entirely appropriate for the primary purpose of public examinations—the provision of qualifications. Sensible assumptions of statistical continuity between adjacent years, taking into account any known changes in the provenance of the candidates, are likely to hold reasonably well because major changes in overall educational standards are unlikely to be rapid. Moreover, although the use of statistical data in the annual awarding process is prey to all the problems discussed earlier in relation to arbitrary choice of reference groups, differential performance by well defined sub-groups and so on, the size of the effects concerned is unlikely to be large between adjacent years. In particular, a new reference group (the previous year's candidates) is used on each occasion. The implication is that standards can be maintained to a reasonably close tolerance between any two adjacent years but that this does not guarantee that standards set, say, 15 years apart are comparable, though they may be. Because the selection processes in which examination results are most important usually involve individuals who were awarded their grades within a few years of each other, the primary role of examinations as qualifications is reasonably secure. The use of examination results as accurate indicators of quantitative changes in educational standards over long time periods is, however, perilous.

Since the assumption of statistical continuity which is made during examination awarding tends to reduce the scale of changes in outcomes which would otherwise result, it could be argued that changes in public examination outcomes reflect long term changes in overall attainment but tend simply to understate them. This argument, of course, depends crucially upon an assumption that there is no long term bias in the process of qualitative judgement of candidates' work and here the socially constructed nature of examination standards is important. The expectations of the examiners who judge the quality of candidates' work are rooted in their professional experience of their own students' attainments, discussion with their colleagues, contact with current educational thinking and, indeed, current political issues and social mores. Clearly, such expectations will not be static but will evolve to reflect changing social and educational influences. Once again, from the long-standing use of public examination grades in educational and vocational selection, it seems reasonable to infer that such dynamic norms, subject to statistical controls, provide standards which are stable enough to underpin useful individual qualifications. It does not follow, however, that they offer a sufficiently constant basis for measuring changes in attainment over long periods of time.

Public Examination Results as Monitors of Educational Standards

To emphasise the points from the preceding section in concrete terms, in this section I will briefly consider the interpretation of some recent historic data.

Figure 6 shows how success rates changed between 1985 and 1995 in a particular assessment. However, before I say whether Figure 6 relates to one or more GCSE or GCE examinations, the reader is invited to

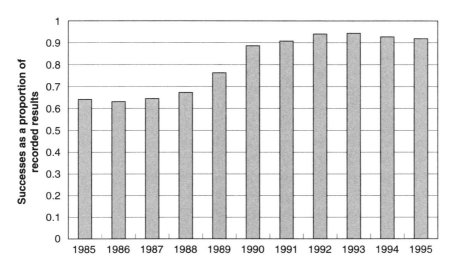

Figure 6. Success rate variations between 1985 and 1995.

pause and consider the question: does the graph indicate a rise in the standards of attainment of the candidates between 1988 and 1992 or a reduction in the assessment demands? Particularly adventurous readers might like to consider whether both effects took place and, if so, what their relative contributions to the overall pattern were.

In fact, Figure 6 shows the proportion of people reaching the summit of Mount Everest, expressed as a proportion of those who reached the summit or died on the mountain.[10] Since Mount Everest has not shrunk significantly in recent years, the interpretation of Figure 6 presumably has to be that people have got better at climbing it. Does this mean that climbing Mount Everest has become less demanding? In one sense, the answer is probably *yes*. For example, better equipment and more thorough preparation based upon the experience of earlier expeditions is likely to have contributed to the improved success rate. Here, then, is a further question to reflect upon: do such improvements represent an improvement in mountaineering standards or not?

Figure 7 shows the national percentage of girls in the Year 11 cohort who were awarded a Grade C or better in GCSE/O-level/CSE English between 1985 and 1995. Hopefully, it is now clear why interpretation of this graph in terms of either falling examination standards or rising attainment is problematic. In the Mount Everest example, appeal to the common human experience that mountains do not normally change height on short time scales enabled us to rule out one interpretation of the data but in the case of examination outcomes there is no such common experience. Thus, the two sides in the annual argument which greets the publication of public examination results about whether educational standards are rising or examination standards are falling are defined by their preconceptions about the relative likelihood of improving educational standards on the one hand or changing examination standards on the other. Since the examination data cannot, themselves, provide evidence one way or the other, they contribute nothing to the debate except a focus for argument. Either interpretation can be defended but neither can be proven without recourse to other information which is both sparse and, itself, controversial. It follows that serious attempts to monitor educational standards quantitatively

---

[10] Data from the New York Times (as reported at http: //everest.mountainzone.com/98/facts.html), un-amended except for the use of a rolling average to remove annual fluctuations caused by the relatively small number of attempts made on the summit of Mount Everest in any one year.

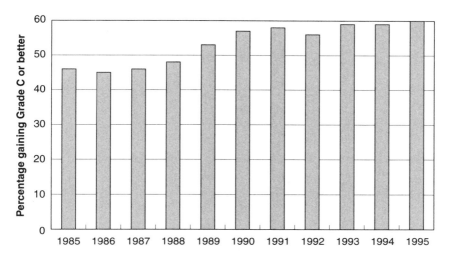

Figure 7. Year 11 girls' pass rates in GCSE/O-level/CSE English 1985–1995. Data from *GCSE Results Analysis: an analysis of the 1985 GCSE results and trensds over time*, published in London by the School Curriculum and Assessment Authority in 1996. (Note that the apparent drop in 1992 coincides with the use of a different original data source for 1992 onwards.)

must use information other than the statistics of public examination results.

Further questions arise in the light of Figure 8 which shows the national percentage of boys in the Year 11 cohort who were awarded a Grade C or better in GCSE/O-level/CSE English between 1985 and 1995. Comparison of Figures 7 and 8 shows that the improvement in boys' reported results was substantially less than that for girls over the time period shown. This raises several new interesting questions such as:

- Are GCSE English examinations increasingly biased in favour of girls or are educational standards for girls improving at a faster rate than those for boys or are there social phenomena leading to a growing gap between the performance of boys and girls or is there some other explanation?

- If the overall pass rate for boys and girls combined had been kept constant from 1985 to 1995, the boys results would have declined, does this mean that boys were really getting worse at English while the girls got better?

The examination results themselves can shed no light on the answers to these questions but it seems worth noting that those who want to

Mike Cresswell

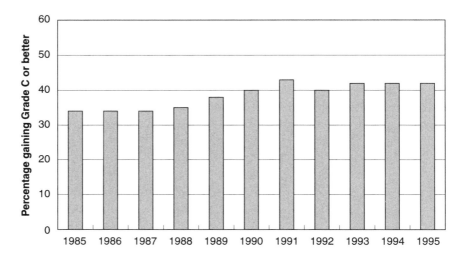

Figure 8. Year 11 boys' pass rates in GCSE/O-level/CSE English 1085–1995. Data again taken from *GCSE Results Analysis: an analysis of the 1985 GCSE results and trensds over time.* (Note that, as in Figure 7, the apparent drop in 1992 coincides with the use of a different original data source for 1992 onwards.)

interpret the data purely in terms of falling examination standards must be able to explain how those standards have fallen more for girls than for boys, even though they have taken identical examinations. In any case, there are many explanations for changes in examination candidates' results, relating to demographic, social and administrative variables, which mean that interpretation of examination statistics *per se* in terms of the quality of education delivered by the school system would still be impossible (see Newton 1997b, for an excellent review of these issues).

What contribution can public examinations make to monitoring standards?

Finally, I want to move away from what some might consider a rather negative analysis to a more positive perspective. I have argued that the objective measurement of changes in educational standards over time is impossible in theory. I have also argued that, even if theoretical concerns are set aside in a pragmatic search for useful, if fallible, quantitative measures of general educational standards, public examinations are not the answer. In particular the procedures used to set standards in public examinations have been developed to produce useful individual qualifications but their results cannot be reliably interpreted as quantitative indicators of long term changes in educational standards.

However, that is not to say that public examinations cannot provide valuable evidence of a qualitative kind about changing educational standards. In particular, past examination syllabuses, question papers, marking schemes and candidates' scripts provide a resource which could be used far more than it is to study the ways in which educational objectives and expectations and, indeed, the attainments of candidates have changed over time. The result of such studies would, of course, be relatively complex qualitative descriptions of change, rather than single headline statistics and such studies would say little about the current effectiveness of educational institutions compared with the effectiveness of comparable institutions in the past. However, rich qualitative descriptions of changing expectations and attainments would more properly reflect the true nature of educational standards and the complexity of the questions implicit in any attempt to monitor them over periods of more than a year or two.

Descriptive monitoring of this kind would, of course, reflect the values of those carrying out the studies and would not be objective but I have already argued that all approaches to monitoring standards involve subjectivity. The analyses would inevitably reflect current values so, if pressed to comparative conclusions, could only ever say that we, today, with our current values, prefer the past or prefer the present. However, are not our present values and beliefs a sufficient basis for action? Indeed, what other basis would we ever want to use? Perhaps the most dangerous aspect of the enterprise is that the result might be used to provide apparently 'scientific' justification for the pursuit of self-serving agendas, based upon idiosyncratic values, which could be claimed by those involved to be as legitimate a basis for action as any other set of values.

The best defence against this possibility is not, however, to deny that qualitative, and necessarily subjective, comparisons over time have any value nor to pretend that objective quantitative comparisons are possible. It is to confront the basic questions: What is the purpose of education? Is it economic success for our country; economic success for our children as individuals; the transmission of our culture; the fullest possible development of each individual's character and talents; or all of these,[11] in which case how do they interact and what relative emphasis should they be given? From these matters we might then move on to look in detail at the nature and degree of the attainments we wish

---

[11] No doubt readers can think of several other candidates.

our children to acquire and begin to develop useful answers to questions about the educational standards to which we aspire. Scrutiny of examination scripts would then be one source of subjective qualitative evidence as to whether our aspirations were being met. However, for the theoretical and practical reasons which I have set out in this paper, the statistics of public examination outcomes cannot, and do not, provide objective or unequivocal quantitative measures of temporal changes in educational standards.

Discussion

John Gray

Introduction

The view that performance in public examinations provides some kind of objective yardstick for judging educational standards is widely held. Examination boards are seen as the main keepers of these standards. Mike Cresswell's observation, therefore, that there is in reality no equivalent of the French metre rule against which to judge educational standards is not simply refreshing in its tacit acknowledgement that the annual debates about standards are flimsily-based. Crucially, he raises questions about how rigorous the practices so-called 'keepers of the standards' adopt to ensure their maintenance actually are and, equally importantly, about what further activities might reasonably be developed with the same aim in mind. His distinctive contribution is to make plain the assumptions underlying current practices—the picture he reveals is simultaneously familiar and disturbing (Cresswell 1998).

Much of Cresswell's paper focuses specifically on 'the maintenance of comparable exam standards between years' and the 'related matter of interpreting changes in the statistics of public examination results over time'. Both questions are central to concerns about maintaining standards. To come to conclusions about such issues exam boards use a mixture of both 'qualitative judgement and statistical data'. Somewhat unusually Cresswell offers accounts of both. His treatment of the statistical issues informing the maintenance of standards is, however, a good deal fuller than his account of the use of qualitative data. This imbalance certainly reflects the weight of the research literature and is, perhaps, inevitable but makes one wonder how exactly potentially conflicting pieces of evidence from the two sources are reconciled.

Maintaining Standards as Social Practice

In the absence of the equivalent of physical yardsticks Cresswell argues that maintaining educational standards is best viewed as a social practice. This is a powerful insight whose implications he explores in some depth. Standards are not maintained by reference to some external yardstick(s) but through the social construction of inter-subjective agreements amongst those most closely involved—and principally the examiners themselves.

'Shared agreements' play a central role in contemporary philosophical thinking about objectivity and the nature of truth. However, a philosophical perspective is clearly not sufficient and needs to be accompanied by a rigorous analysis of the social practices employed to maintain standards. Who is recruited to be an examiner and who is promoted within the system to more senior positions? How are new recruits inducted and existing examiners refreshed? Crucially, since the system depends on the belief not merely that shared judgements are possible but that they actually exist, what does the evidence suggest about the extent of initial agreement amongst examiners? And, given these starting points, to what extent do the various processes to which exam boards then subject their examiners increase the likelihood of so-called agreements? In philosophical terms such judgements are likely to be most 'objective' when they are reached by 'unforced' processes.

Few of these issues have, to date, been researched in any depth. Only occasional glimpses are available about how examining committees conduct their business. There is, however, a more fundamental hurdle to be overcome. The idea that an exam board 'maintains standards' over time is almost certainly so integral to its culture and functioning that it seems doubtful whether any individual board could reach anything other than an essentially positive assessment of its own contribution. Some intensive analysis of how a board responded during those episodes when there was some possibility of 'breaking frame' would be necessary to cast light on this issue. But, frustratingly, such instances would themselves probably be dismissed as 'exceptional' by those most closely involved.

In sum, whilst there might be some value in exploring those occasions where an exam board was not maintaining standards from year to year (or in danger of not doing so) the low incidence of such events would scarcely constitute independent evidence. As Cresswell argues, if one accepts that examination standards are 'socially constructed' then their legitimacy is based on the willingness of 'students, parents, teachers, employers and policy-makers' to 'accept the competence of the judges'. He suggests that 'the competence of those who set standards is more likely to be accepted if the procedures used are transparent and public knowledge' but the maintenance of trust is the key. It must be recognised that one of the reasons why there is still relatively little research on the maintenance of standards as a social practice is that such evidence might itself damage public confidence rather than reinforce it.

Statistical Contributions to Maintaining Standards

Over the last decade, as Cresswell demonstrates, exam boards have adopted increasingly sophisticated statistical procedures to explore standards-related issues. Their basic analytical armoury, however, has remained largely unchanged—namely what happened last year. There are good reasons for this of course. Last year's results are 'secure' in several respects: the pool of candidates taking any particular exam, for example, is likely to be fairly similar; the majority of examiners will probably have been involved the previous year and probably have set similar kinds of questions; the curriculum being examined can be assumed to bear comparison over such a short passage of time; and, perhaps as importantly bearing in mind the need to inspire public confidence, in the great majority of cases the published results will have been accepted subject only to a few marginal appeals. The cumulative effect of this reasoning is to reinforce the view that what happened last year provides a good starting point.

In the circumstances it is hardly surprising that what seems like a valid set of assumptions become translated into a set of working practices. Cresswell suggests that there are just three arguments that any particular group of examiners can employ to explain and justify changes from last year's results. These are that:

1 as a whole, the candidates as a group are simply better (or worse) than last year's;

2 the balance of centre types and/or genders has changed; or

3 this year's new (or missing) candidates are better (or worse) than the rest.

What is striking about all three explanations is how little additional evidence examiners are offered to inform their judgements. No evidence is offered, for example, with respect to the first explanation about whether this year's candidates have performed better/worse than last year's on some other (related) measure of performance on some previous occasion. The assumption is that they are basically the same unless there is powerful evidence to suggest otherwise. However, from Cresswell's account it would appear that no routine attempts are made to check out whether this assumption is valid.

Whilst examiners are offered evidence on the changing balance of centre types and gendered entries, the assumption is again that variations in performance between years will be small. the this year/last year frame of reference reinforces this impression. Cresswell comments that 'about 75% of centres entering candidates in any one year also entered candidates for the same examination in the previous year' and sees this as supporting judgements about the stability of the pool of candidates. Yet it is obvious that across three years the changes could be more substantial. If, as he suggests, around 75% of the centres one year are present the next then it is possible that in the third year only 56% of the original centres will remain.

Similar considerations could apply to the third explanation which Cresswell sees as a variant of the second. Examiners seem to make essentially optimistic assumptions about the extent of stability amongst pools of candidates drawn from different years. In the past, when only a minority of pupils were entered for any public examinations, the assumption that the pool of comparably-qualified candidates might have expanded could have been tenable; this seems less likely, however, when almost all pupils are entered for some examinations. In the circumstances it is hardly surprising if much of the examiners' practice seems like informed guesswork reinforced by (some) statistical insights.

Further Factors Contributing to Change

Over the last decade the proportions of young people securing 5 or more grade A–C passes in the 16+ examinations has been rising year-on-year at historically unprecedented rates. How, some critics ask, can these changes be squared with the maintenance of standards? The introduction of the new GCSE examination in 1988 (replacing the old bi-partite system of GCEs and CSEs) undoubtedly contributed to the process. Changes in examiners' assumptions and practices over the same period may also have fuelled the rises. At the same time, however, there are two further sets of explanations which exam boards have historically defined as beyond their control and consequently scarcely consider at all.

First, the social composition of the pupil population has been changing. Better-educated parents have created higher expectations of performance, disadvantaged groups typically associated with lower performance have declined in size and young people themselves appear to have become increasingly motivated to take (and do well) in public exams. During the last decade the social significance of the 16+ examinations has also changed. In a situation where the majority of young people now stay on after their period of compulsory schooling has ended, one of the key function of public examinations may have changed—the securing of 5 or more high grade passes becomes simply a stepping stone to the next stage.

Second, the climate within which schools find themselves operating has been transformed. In particular, they have been encouraged in recent years to 'improve' their pupils' exam performances (Gray *et al.* 1999). Schools have consequently adopted a variety of strategies. They have, for example, entered more pupils for more examinations; identified and focused their efforts on 'borderline' candidates (mostly at the crucial grade D/grade C boundary); provided more support for pupils to revise and hone their exam techniques; and, on occasion, exploited the opportunities to select exam boards likely to give them the most favourable grades. In the process they have gnawed away at the edges of some of the exam boards' core assumptions. Even if, as seems likely, examiners are increasingly aware of some of these influences they appear to have few, if any, ways of taking them systematically into account.

Finally, there are a set of factors related to the examiners' own behaviour. Cresswell suggests that 'fluctuations in the standards represented by (examiners') qualitative judgements' may contribute to differences in exam outcomes. In other words, even when groups of examiners think in similar ways, they may implement their shared assumptions in somewhat different ways. Other factors may also be influential, however, even when exam boards are broadly aware of them. The changeover from one chief examiner in any particular subject to another, for example, could be a time of disjuncture as could other factors influencing the recruitment of particular cohorts of examiners. An unusually large number of appeals in the previous year or extensive criticism of current standards may create a climate for the next year. And the fluctuating fortunes of different subjects as they 'compete' for pupils, with some rising and others falling in popularity, may also feed into the process. Differences between exam boards may also need to be brought into the reckoning. It is incumbent upon exam board officials to claim that such factors have been taken into account; unfortunately it is not always clear how they have done so.

Concluding Thoughts

The procedures currently adopted by exam boards to 'maintain standards' from one year to the next are fairly limited. They clearly take steps to use such evidence as they have readily to hand to inform their judgements. Indeed, within their own terms and as working hypotheses across short spans of years, such approaches can probably be said to work. During periods of rapid change, however, some of their assumptions are likely to break down. It needs to be acknowledged that the quest for truly 'objective' standards is illusory. Nonetheless, the challenge to existing practices thrown down by Cresswell's paper is clear. Should exam boards' efforts to 'maintain standards' continue to be almost entirely self-referencing? Or is it time to consider the introduction of a wider range of external evidence?

Lindsay Paterson

Introduction

Mike Cresswell's paper is a definitive demonstration that judgement is unavoidable when assessing standards. I have no disagreement with that. But I would take issue with the implications which his paper briefly indicates. At several points, he draws a sharp distinction between objectivity and judgement. Indeed he says that 'examination standards . . . cannot be made objective'.

My main point is that judgement is not just subjective. Judgement is socially constructed—as Cresswell acknowledges but does not develop—and as such can be the basis of social research. Moreover, that research into the social basis of judgement can be every bit as rigorous as the statistical analysis of examination results. In fact, it can be every bit as statistical as well.

Knowledge is Socially Constructed

So my first point is that judgement is not subjective. If it is not objective, then it is at least inter-subjective. Not being a philosopher, I am not really in a position to provide a full philosophical analysis of this debate. But I would make three points:

1 There are now many reasons to question the logical positivist claim that everything which is not observable (or derived from a priori reasoning) is mere opinion (Barnes 1974, Berger and Luckmann 1966, Hollis and Lukes 1982, Kuhn 1970, Lakatos 1974).

2 Being a sociologist rather than a philosopher- and being, moreover, a Scottish sociologist—I turn for guidance on this to the Scottish Enlightenment. A central theme of the Enlightenment's epistemology was to distinguish between judgement and mere opinion. For example, here is how Christopher Berry (1997) has recently characterised Adam Smith's view of the matter: 'through our imagination we are able to conceive what we would feel if we were in the situation of another' (p. 162). Smith called this 'sympathy'. As a result, 'individuals identify themselves with the "impartial spectator"' (p. 164)

3 And then we can find that theme appearing specifically in writing about statistical epistemology, for example in Ian Hacking's argument that the reason why we accept statistical method at all is social convention (Hacking 1965: 52, 226–7). An example is in the apparently arbitrary levels of statistical significance with which we are accustomed to operating, at least informally: Hacking's point is that these levels still matter, despite their arbitrariness, precisely because they have been so widely used in practice by natural and social scientists. And he cites C. S. Peirce arguing that, to make sense of statistical inference at all, we have to align our own interests with those of the whole community (Hacking 1990: 211).

The Social Uses of Credentials

The next point, then, concerns the implications of knowledge's being socially constructed. It follows that I am in complete agreement with Cresswell that norm-referencing is unavoidable. Attempts to establish criteria of assessment can work only locally, as it were, because the *selection* of criteria is socially conditioned. For example, our societies seem to be coming to the firm consensus that basic IT skills have to be acquired by everyone who could reasonably call themselves educated.

So that looks like a criterion. But the selection of that criterion is a matter of social judgement: there is nothing absolutely compelling about any particular level of IT skill. After all, just a few years ago, the criteria of what is required would have been quite different. The same point about the social selection of criteria can be made about other topics that might appear to be criteria—for example, learning to recite the Lord's Prayer or doing long division by hand.

Moreover, just as choosing criteria for assessment is socially conditioned, so too are the uses to which public examinations are put. Whatever educationalists might prefer in the way of criterion-referencing, we cannot get away from the social sorting role of public examinations—an aspect of what Randall Collins (1979) calls credentialism. It is not for reasons of obtuseness that employers or university selectors continue to insist on having ways of ranking applicants, and it is not unreasonable that they turn to public examinations as a first, crude measure of the rank order.

So, if norms and social sorting are inescapable, the questions for social research are things like this:

- on what grounds are the norms socially acceptable at any particular time?
- how do one set of norms lose social acceptability?
- how are new norms established?

Another way of putting this is to see the entire enterprise of public examinations as a vast piece of research in itself, which has as its primary social aim the discovery of the most effective way of allocating people to social roles, and of equipping them to move among social roles. So—translating the questions I have just asked into the language of research design—the problem is to establish the validity of this vast bit of research:

- do the examinations validly measure things which society judges to be worth measuring?
- does the examination system respond to changes in these social judgements about what is worth measuring?
- does society have ways of altering the examination system to incorporate new judgements?

An Illustration: Scotland

Establishing the validity of the research project of public examinations would itself require several large research projects. Let me illustrate the potential, however, by the instance of Scotland. Despite what Cresswell implicitly claims, his paper is not about Britain at all. It is about England, or maybe England and Wales. Indeed, I guess that a meeting such as that held at the British Academy in October 1998 could not have taken place in the same form in Scotland, because public examinations there have been subjected to far fewer criticisms and doubts than they have been in England.

That is partly a historical point. Scots quite like meritocratic selection, and have done so for at least a century. But it is also a more recent one. The crisis of confidence in standards has simply not affected Scottish debate to nearly the same extent as in England. Trying to use social research to understand why matters are different in Scotland can point to some features that would be needed in a programme of research on the social origins and development of standards. I cite this research, not to imply complacency about Scottish standards, but simply to illustrate how we might conduct research on the social acceptance of standards. My point is not to try to show that standards in Scotland really are higher or lower than in England, but to give examples of research that might be relevant to understanding the social basis of trust in current standards, whatever they may be.

To start with, let me note the evidence that there is no public sense of crisis. Repeated social surveys have shown that around two thirds to three quarters of the general population believe:

- that comprehensive secondary education is effective (as shown by analysis of the 1997 British Election Survey reported in Brown *et al.* (1999), by analysis of the British Social Attitudes Surveys reported by Arnott (1993) and by Paterson (1997), and by analysis of a poll conducted in 1996 by System 3 reported by Paterson (1997));
- that it teaches the basics well (as shown by analysis of the British Social Attitudes Surveys reported by Arnott (1993) and by Paterson (1997), and by analysis of the poll conducted in 1996 by System 3 reported by Paterson (1997));
- and that standards are not falling (as shown by a poll conducted by ICM for *The Scotsman* (1998));

One of the reasons for this belief is probably the research which has been carried out on the specific judgements made by individual examiners. The most notable example is the investigation by the Scottish Council for Research in Education in 1996 into the standards of the Higher Grade examinations (Devine *et al.* 1996). That was commissioned by a Conservative-controlled Scottish Office, and had as one of its effects the removal of the issue of examination standards from serious political debate. Over time, a more important source of research than the SCRE project has probably been the research which has been conducted by the former Scottish Examinations Board itself (now the Scottish Qualifications Authority). For example, since the late 1970s, it has monitored standards by statistical techniques devised by Alison Kelly (1976), essentially using factor analysis to study the relative difficulty of examinations in each subject in each year, and then allowing the conclusions to inform the setting of next year's papers. The Board and Authority have also retained a random sample of scripts in each subject at each level in each year to allow retrospective checking of standards (which was how the SCRE research was possible).

Most importantly of all, however, several programmes of research now offer explanations of the rise in examination attainment. This research is relevant in this context because it presents plausible explanations of these changes that do not depend on claiming a fall in assessment standards. Thus the research has helped to support the claim that the examinations are performing the purposes that society wants them to perform. This research addresses only one aspect of what would have to be addressed in a full programme of research into the social basis of examination standards: it addresses the question of validity—of whether the examinations continue to perform the selection functions that society wants of them. The research does not address, for example, the question of *how* standards are developed or change.

Four points emerge from that research on why examination attainment has risen. The first and most important is the second-generation effect of rising educational capital (Burnhill *et al.* 1990, Paterson 1992). Put simply: the children of better-educated parents do better, and there are a lot more better educated parents around now than there were thirty years ago.

Second, if we ask why today's parents started liking school two decades or so ago, Scottish research provides us with quite a specifically Scottish answer: comprehensive secondary schools (Benn and Chitty

1996, McPherson and Willms 1987). The evidence from research is that they did indeed partly (but only partly) fulfil one of the intentions of their founders, of tapping into educational talent in social groups which had previously been wholly excluded.

Third, comprehensive inclusion of the working class was made easier to achieve politically by the fact that these same disadvantaged social groups were declining in size (Paterson 1995). This purely demographic trend was intensified by social mobility—parents moving out of working-class occupations into middle-class ones, and their children then acquiring the educational characteristics of the middle class in general.

The fourth point is about how demand for education can be stimulated (Paterson 1992, Robertson 1992). Scottish research has shown that young people respond to what is on offer in higher education, and are motivated to attempt and pass examinations in order to take advantage of what is on offer. There is no 'fixed pool' of demand. And the same can be said in the post-compulsory stages of schooling (Paterson and Raffe 1995). Reforms to curriculum and assessment in the last four years of Scottish schooling have contributed to stimulating demand, by making these school years more enjoyable.

I have gone through this research-based explanation of rising attainment in order to indicate what research can do—what it can show about the validity of the public examinations as selection mechanisms. The research shows that there are good, sensible, and rigorously established reasons why young people are doing better, and so that panic about a crisis of standards is simply unnecessary. I should say also that all the research I have cited has been statistical, most of it using quite complex methods of analysis.

But even that research would not have been compelling if there had not been popular faith in the system. Education is regarded as a key Scottish civic institution (Paterson 1998; forthcoming); there is a long-standing trust in meritocratic selection as a fair and effective form of social organisation (Anderson 1995, Gray *et al.* 1983, Smith and Hamilton 1980); there is quite widespread trust in teachers' capacity to make the system and the selection mechanism work (as shown by the poll conducted by ICM for *The Scotsman* (1998)); and the system is trusted to reform itself to meet new demands (as shown, for example, by the near-unanimous view that decisions about Scottish educational policy should be taken in Scotland: see data from ICM reported in *The Scotsman* (1998)). The educational research I have rehearsed has probably helped to establish and maintain that trust.

The trust creates a social climate in which a principle of parsimony excludes an explanation in terms of declining standards. Provided there are adequate other explanations of rising attainment, the socially and politically inconvenient option of doubting standards is simply not needed. Whether that basis of trust will survive the creation of the Scottish parliament in 1999 remains to be seen. It could well be that a parliament with democratic legitimacy will erode the popular confidence which Scottish civic institutions have been able to command in the Union. (For a discussion of this, see Paterson (1998).) The point for us, though, is the methodological one that the same processes of social research would be able to measure a decline of trust as have been used to investigate its social basis hitherto.

Conclusion

Contrasting Scotland to England (and maybe Wales) points to the kind of research which could be done to find out what the necessary conditions are for the social acceptability of an examination system: that is, in relation to Cresswell's 'value judgements', establishing what their social origins are and what are their mechanisms of change. My methodological point, for academics and policy makers, is that doing this research is not at all an attempt to escape from the rigour of analysing examination statistics. If anything, the complexity of this task makes it rather more methodologically demanding than annually perusing the tables of crude examination pass rates.

A. H. (Chelly) Halsey

Mike Cresswell has written a splendid paper arguing that under the debate on *educational* standards lies a more technical and philosophical controversy about the reliability and validity of public *examination* standards. He points to research evidence on the fragility of long-term comparisons of examination standards, to the shifting perspectives of the guardians of those standards, the changing pressures from the interested parties and the rising intervention of the State. He argues that, in the end, it is all based, however rationally, on value judgement. I agree with him, but with modification.

First examinations, while often used, as he asserts, 'to provide information for future meritocratic educational and vocational selection decisions' are also vital tests of competence, for example in the safe driving of cars or in surgery on human beings. The language of value judgement, other than universal accord that road accidents are to be avoided and human life preserved, is perhaps less relevant in such cases. The essential point of the examination for a driver or a doctor is to establish not who is better than whom but rather who can perform the job adequately. The task, in other words, is a classification of competence, not an ordinal ranking of competitors. From that point of view modern and future society may be deemed to need examinations for efficiency rather than for selection.

Second, again though I agree that debate over educational standards is underpinned by one over examination standards, I would make the sociological point that tests of competence to perform *any role* are part and parcel of social arrangements. They are by no means confined to formal schooling. For example monarchs and the inheritors of businesses reach their positions through 'ascription' but it should also be noted that 'achievement' is added to ascription as part of the expected preparation for the role, involving subjection to the exhausting ritual round of royal appearances in the one case and workshop experience, business school training etc. in the other. Examination may simply follow the rules of inheritance at death in either case, but the examination also involves abdication or bankruptcy with parliament or the receiver as examiners. Exploration of these complicated forms of ascription and achievement and their interactions would take us extensively beyond the limits of Cresswell's paper. It would, for example, raise questions of whether there should be examinations in capacity for parenthood and, if so, whether this preparatory education should be located in schools.

Third, however, I want to take up and elaborate Cresswell's insistence on the function of examinations for selection, whether meritocratic or otherwise, and illustrate it critically by reference to the expansion of higher education in the UK especially in 1992. Societies in general live by rewarding role players with money, honours, privileges etc and by punishing failure with imprisonment, demotion, removal of licence to practice a qualification, and many other kinds of disesteem. Against this background the universities have to be seen as loci of honours and privileges but in addition as emerging centres of the economy, the polity and society. Standards must therefore be maintained as to student entry, certification at exit, appointment and promotion of staff, and efficiency of learning and discovery.

Now all the conditions of supply and demand have been changing rapidly with respect to further and higher education over the past thirty years i.e. since the Robbins Report. The proportion of the relevant age group entering universities has multiplied ten fold since before the second world war and is now one third. On a still more long-range perspective there are now at least three times as many university teachers as there were students (20,000) at the beginning of the century. In 1985 11 per cent of the seventeen year old population obtained 3 or more A level passes. By 1995 this figure had doubled to 22%. Can it be concluded that standards of entry are declining or that there has been grade dilution (inflation)?

Cresswell, if I understand him, replies that the question cannot be answered and offers several technical reasons. By contrast the Dearing Committee (Dearing 1995) (with no discernible expertise of the kind amply demonstrated by Cresswell) concluded that there was no basis for the view that entry via A level to higher education had become significantly easier. Nevertheless it must be noted that in the same year the pass rate at A level rose again for the 16th year in succession, though the proportion of A's at A level levelled off. In 1998 the performance rate continued to climb but only just. From the standpoint of political and social function the reactions were highly if cynically predictable. The government congratulated itself for its reforms and commended teachers and candidates for their hard work, the teacher unions celebrated rising productivity and demanded increased pay, the opposition suspected falling standards in the shape of grade inflation.

Given the speed of expansion, conflict comes as no surprise. It expresses itself in diverse challenges to authority: for example over anonymity of refereeing papers submitted to journals for publication, or over judging applications for appointment or promotion, or over the validity of league tables, or over the award of ranks by central agencies to particular university departments. In short, the rapid replacement of tiny, consensual and élite universities by mass systems of higher education, whatever its great merits, leads to the decline of trust and to demand for greater openness in decision making.

But let us focus on matriculation—the conditions of entry into universities. The USA, leading an expansionist field, was first also in developing national standardised attainment tests. Each European country has a specific national educational qualification which forms the main basic requirement for entry to higher education. The qualification generally covers at least five subjects, some compulsory, and usually including mathematics, the native language and one foreign modern language. England, Wales and Northern Ireland are unusual in limiting the number of subjects more narrowly and thus specialising earlier. At least five passes at GCE (usually taken at age 16) are required for degree level courses, of which two must be of Advanced level (usually taken at 18), although most candidates for entry attempt three A level subjects and already have at least 6 O-level passes. There is a passionate controversy over the special position of the A level examination in England, which guards entry to the university as does the abitur and the baccalauriat in Germany, France and elsewhere. Behind it lie the status and class battles for possession of educational property which have been intensified by the reform and expansion movements of the period since World War II. Special arrangements meanwhile exist for the growing body of mature students and those lacking 'traditional' qualifications.

In East and West Europe generally the state has increasingly controlled entry to higher education since Napoleonic times, either through defining examination content and standards or through varied means of student financial support or through special schemes of encouragement for particular social categories of student by positive discrimination or, more usually, by setting up barriers to entry. In the West some countries like Belgium, France or Germany used one uniform national examination. Sweden attempted the ranking of students by marks weighted according to the courses taken and work experience (which tacitly modifies age as a selective barrier). Positive discrimination in favour of candidates with working class backgrounds has been used in Poland and Czechoslovakia, as well as in Hungary, though examination performance has also been part of the entrance procedure. Entrance examinations have been widely used with higher requirements in medicine, science and law. Such procedures obtain not only in the highly prestigious institutions such as Oxford and Cambridge in England and the Grandes Ecoles in France, but also in the East European former Communist states where, at least a quarter of the places were reserved for working-class students. Even the lottery is not unknown. In the Netherlands the problem of excessive demand was overcome by its use. A lottery was operated in which an individual's chances were weighted by marks attained in the secondary school leaving examinations.

Nevertheless the automatic right of entry to the university which is the traditional privilege of those who obtain a baccalaureat or the abitur, still gives admission in France and Italy, though not to other forms of higher education. The consequences are seen in high failure or dropout rates in the first two years of undergraduate study. We have here essentially a form of retrospective examination by actual performance 'on the job'. Even in England and Scotland this phenomenon has appeared since the expansion of the universities to include the former polytechnics in 1992. It is an inevitable consequence of the transformation to mass higher education. In other words it is possible to use the first one or two years of university study as a selective device in place of the traditional matriculation examinations of the upper secondary school. It is therefore not surprising that as late as 1994 there was fear of rioting in Paris and reports of long queues for admission in Bologna. Other countries, like Belgium or Spain, never granted the prerogatives of the abitur. In France, however, in spite of several university reforms, including the Loi Savary of 1984, the right of entry of a bachelier has never been modified. Of course, the highly selective Grandes Ecoles continue to cream off the best 15 per cent or so of the candidates. And the *numerus clausus* has been increasingly applied in France and Germany so that we can now describe the right as nominal. It does not guarantee a place in any particular faculty of any particular university.

In summary it appears that the evolution of matriculation and the admissions system in recent decades has been to move the point of selection upwards from the upper secondary school and its examinations to the admissions offices of the institutions of higher education. The traditional system was essentially controlled by teachers in universities. Control now is much more in the hands of politicians and budgetary administrators. Diversity is to be found at both the secondary and tertiary levels and the unique role of the baccalaureat, the abitur and their equivalents in other European countries as the *rite de passage* to university education, is no more.

Instead there have developed alternative modes of entry to a diverse set of post-compulsory educational and training institutions with the parallel development of vocational equivalents to A level, the baccalaureat and the abitur. In France there is a technical baccalaureat with 12 options as well as the traditional one with 8 sections and a proposed 30 option practical baccalaureat which, it is expected, will be taken in one form or another by 80 per cent of the secondary school leavers by the end of the century. Dr Cresswell's warnings against the comparability of examinations in different subjects are thus alarmingly compounded.

In most countries most students first enter full-time higher education aged between 18 and 21. At the end of the nineteen eighties the rate
of full-time enrolment in this age group was more than ten per cent in
over half of the OECD countries. However, older students are also
admitted everywhere; in Germany a quota of places is reserved for
them. In the Nordic countries, Austria, West Germany and Switzerland
full time enrolment in 1990 was higher among persons aged 22 to 25
than among those aged 18 to 21. Reasons for starting first study in
higher education later in life are many; some students pursue lower level
further education full-time or enter employment; others may retake
entry examinations and so increase the range of institutions which
will accept them.

All in all then it appeared by the nineteen nineties that the articula-
tion of the formal education system to the labour market in Europe was
entering a new state of flux. It was not only that the macro-economic
management associated with Keynes, Bretton Woods, and the left-wing
planning governments of the nineteen fifties and sixties was collapsing.
Nor was it only that the command economies of Eastern Europe were
rapidly eroded at the end of the eighties. It was also that the sexual
division of labour was now being comprehensively renegotiated, that
the 'career' to which university admission had been traditionally a key
with its life-long employment in a superior trade or profession, was
disappearing. Part-time and temporary contracts were becoming normal, and not only for casual, unskilled and unschooled work but for
professional and technical appointments. Europe, along with the rest of
the advanced industrial world, was entering a profoundly different
phase of the development of its economy and society and therefore of
its educational arrangements.

The Measurement of Standards

DAVID J. BARTHOLOMEW

The Concept of a Standard

STANDARDS ARE AT THE HEART of current educational debates and, if we examine the contexts in which the term is used, we find that the concept is essentially quantitative. Standards are spoken of as high or low and institutions and individuals are ranked according to the level of achievement. Yet, in spite of the ubiquity of the term, there is no simple measuring instrument we can take to a child or a school and read off the appropriate value. Neither is there any natural unit of measurement as there is with some physical quantities. Indeed, the more closely we analyse the concept, the more elusive it seems to be. We find ourselves in the position of St Augustine who is reported to have said of time 'What is time? If no one asks I know, but if I have to say what it is to one who asks, I know not'. Much the same could be said of standards.

The situation we have described is not uncommon in the social sciences; indeed it could be argued that it is the norm. Many of the key variables which occur in the discourse of the social sciences have the characteristic that they cannot be directly observed. Conservatism, alienation, attitude to abortion are further examples of things which are spoken of as if they were real quantities, yet they are not open to direct observation. The abilities and skills with which educational measurement is concerned are of just this kind. In the language of statistics they are latent variables because they are thought of as under-lying, and influencing, the world of observation but are not, themselves, directly accessible to observation.

Before we can begin to provide a conceptual framework for

Proceedings of the British Academy, **102**, 121–150. © The British Academy 2000.

approaching the measurement of standards, we need to note that the term *standard* is used in a variety of senses and these need to be disentangled if confusion is to be avoided. All of them have something to do with levels of achievement, or performance, by children, students or institutions. The standard reached by a student at the end of a course, for example, is thought of as a point on a scale of performance which can be compared with that of other students or with some threshold for passing an examination or achieving a degree of a particular class. Here we are speaking of an *individual* scale which measures the performance of a person.

We also use the term in a collective sense to apply to *groups* of individuals, as when we use it of a school. School league tables are intended to rank schools according to their institutional achievements. Usually this will be done by aggregating the individual performances of the members of the institution by quoting, for example, the proportion who achieve certain A-level grades. These may then be combined with other, similar, measures to form a composite index. But in essence, institutional measures are derived from those pertaining to their members.

Thus whether we are primarily interested in *individual* level or *institutional* level measures, we have to begin with the problem of measuring the performance of individuals.

We have spoken of what is to be measured as performance or achievement because this, as we shall see, is what we actually attempt to measure in practice. But levels of performance are determined by a great variety of factors, some of which may be regarded as more fundamental and important. A parent choosing a school may regard the school's position in the league table as saying something about the quality of its educational provision. A university selecting a student may look at that individual's performance and interpret it as a measure of innate ability or potential. In both cases the data on which the choice is made is the same, yet they are being taken as indicative of quite different things. In reality of course, we know that things are much more complicated. Not only are there other factors which affect performance, such as home background, but those factors may interact with one another, meaning that the effect of one will depend on the others which are present. Thus whatever more fundamental latent variables underlie the score which traditional testing produces, their interpretation is not likely to be straightforward. There is an excellent account of the way in which factors of this kind interact in Johnson

(1997) and the ensuing discussion. This is set in the context of the grade point average system used in American universities but the issue at stake is of much wider relevance.

With that warning of difficulties which lie ahead, we now turn to consider how we can extract a scale of measurement from the assortment of test scores which form the empirical bedrock of the exercise.

The Common Sense Approach

Suppose that n individuals are required to take an examination consisting of p questions, or items. A mark of some kind will be awarded to each answer and the results may then be set out in a table as follows.

There is one column for each item and one row for each individual. (Henceforth we use the terms *item* and *individual* as generic terms). The x's in the body of the table represent the marks awarded and their subscripts specify the row and column, respectively, in which they occur. In the simplest case they may record whether the item was right or wrong; 1 if the answer is correct and 0 if it is wrong. Or they may be marks awarded out of 100, or 20. The items may be questions in a degree examination paper, in which case their number may be as small as 4 or 5, or they may be multiple choice questions running to 50 or even a 100. The items may be sub-divided according to subject or date taken. Individuals may be classified according to school, age or any number of other relevant attributes. Some of the cells may be empty, as when candidates are not required to answer all questions. However, the important thing for our purposes is the near universality of this method of setting out the results of examinations. There must be countless

Table 1. The layout of a typical test result.

	Items				
Individuals	1	2	3	. . . . . .	p
1	x_{11}	x_{12}	x_{13}	. . . . . .	x_{1p}
2	x_{21}	x_{22}	x_{23}	. . . . . .	x_{2p}
3	x_{31}	x_{32}	x_{33}	. . . . . .	x_{3p}
.	.	.	.	.	.
.	.	.	.	.	.
.	.	.	.	.	.
n	x_{n1}	x_{n2}	x_{n3}	. . . . . .	x_{np}

examples in the records of teachers and examining boards of all kinds. The information about performance is contained in the numbers in such tables and the statistical problem is how to extract it.

The following questions arise.

1 How should the items be selected—how many and of what kind?

2 What population of individuals are we interested in? Should we test them all or only a sample? If the latter, how should it be selected?

3 How should the numbers in any row of the table be combined to give a valid measure of the individual's performance?

There are other questions, such as what we can learn from the numbers in the columns of the table about the suitability of the items (e.g. were they too hard or too easy), but we shall concentrate on the three listed above and, especially, on the last.

The choice of items is usually a matter for the judgement of examiners who would be expected to ensure that the syllabus was adequately covered, that the items were of the right 'standard', that they covered the range of skill expected, and so on. Selection of individuals would only arise in large scale investigations, perhaps on a national basis. But if there is no sampling in that sense there are more subtle questions concerning the variation in response one might obtain from one occasion to another with the same individual.

So far as combining the scores in any row of the table to give an index of performance is concerned, the usual practice is to add them up. The row totals, or their averages, have traditionally been seen as the main, if not the only, relevant summary measurement. In the 'right'/ 'wrong' case the total is simply the number correct. Sometimes this may be modified by weighting the individual marks before totalling them or, for example, by selecting only the best q out of p. But that adding up is the sensible thing to do seems to be a matter of common sense.

The central question to be considered later is whether this intuition is well-founded but, in the meantime, a bridge to the theory to follow can be established by probing the matter a little further. We recognise that testing is an uncertain business. We can only use a relatively small number of items in the test and these will, inevitably, give an incomplete picture of the individual's knowledge. Individuals have good and bad days and their answers will reflect not only their knowledge but also their particular circumstances at the time. Response will also depend on the quality of teaching, general educational provision and examination technique. Any particular x in the table can thus be thought of as partly measuring what it is intended to measure and partly the effects of all the extraneous and irrelevant factors such as those listed above. If we think of these two components as additive we are saying that

observed score = true score + deviation.

Our intuition that it is a good thing to add up scores then derives from the fact that we feel the 'deviations' ought, in some sense, to 'cancel out'. The more items we have, the more confident we are likely to feel that the vagaries of the examining procedure will be damped out. Crude though it may seem this simple idea, that an observed score is made up of two parts, a real 'signal' and irrelevant 'noise', is the kernel of the modern statistical approach to the measurement of latent variables.

The Modelling Approach

We now explain how a probability modelling approach tackles the problem. Our aim will be to give a non-technical account which conveys the basic ideas without resort to mathematics. Those who can cope with the mathematics will find a more adequate treatment in Bartholomew (1996) or Bartholomew and Knott (1999).

A statistical model is a mathematical specification of the way in which the observed data are supposed to have been generated. In the present case it will have to describe the linkages between the observed scores—the x's—and the underlying latent variable. It will need to be a probability model in order to incorporate the element of chance which interposes itself between the true performance level of the individual and what we observe. Once this is done it is a matter of statistical routine to infer what can be said about the latent variable.

It is important to understand what the role of the mathematics is. It does not add anything to the data. Rather it expresses in precise terms how we conceive the data to have arisen and places at our disposal a powerful tool for consistent reasoning.

The logic of a modelling exercise is as follows.

1 We entertain the possibility that individuals may be meaningfully located at points along a scale which we identify with level of performance.

2 We specify a plausible mechanism linking an individual's position on the scale with their scores on the items in a test.

3 We deduce observational consequences of our assumptions under **1** and **2** in order to check whether theory and observation agree.

4 If they do we proceed, as if the model were correct, to make deductions about where to place an individual on the scale given their score.

The model tells us what scores to expect for a given value of the latent variable. We then use probability theory to reverse this process and deduce what latent scale position we would expect for a given set of scores.

There is a weak link in the logic of using a model in this way which is often overlooked but which is particularly important in latent variable modelling. Even if the predictions of the model agree well with observation it does not follow that the model is 'true' in any sense. All that we can say is that people behave *as if* it were true. It may be that there are other models which make the same, or almost the same, predictions. If that is the case we have no empirical way of distinguishing between the competing models.

There are many models used in the field of measurement and their forms depend on the kind of data we have. For example, *item response theory* (IRT) models are for binary items where answers are simply right or wrong. Such a model specifies how the chance of getting an item correct depends on the ability of the individual. Again, if the test scores are expressed on a continuous scale, it may be appropriate to treat them as normally distributed, and then to assume that their relationship with ability is that of simple linear regression. In that case we have a special case of *factor analysis*. The only evidence we can have for any such assumption is obtained retrospectively when we check whether its consequences are borne out in practice.

Given the uncertainties, we cannot expect to determine an individual's position on the latent scale precisely. Within the modelling framework we express our uncertainty about the scale value by a probability distribution and, in particular, by its location and dispersion. Thus we aim to say that if a person's test scores are such and such then we 'estimate' their true position to be P, say, with standard deviation S.

It turns out that we can only do this if we know the distribution of the latent variable in the population from which our n individuals are drawn (known as the *prior* distribution). In the nature of the case this is impossible because, if we cannot even observe the latent variable, we certainly cannot know what its distribution is. We therefore appear to be at an impasse but, rather surprisingly, it can be circumvented. If we make rather weak assumptions about the class of models to be used—which includes most of those in common use—nearly all of what we need is unaffected by the choice of prior distribution. In fact, we can invoke the statistical notion of *sufficiency* to show that the prior distribution needed for determining the scale value (called the posterior distribution) depends on the observed scores only through a single statistic. In other words, all the information in the observed scores about the latent variable is contained in this single function. It is remarkable that for one of the main IRT models, as well as for the factor model and many others, this single function turns out to be a weighted sum. There is, therefore, a theoretical basis for what common sense seemed to require. But beyond that the theory also provides a means of determining what the weights should be.

Another consequence of the general theory is that, because of the arbitrariness of the prior distribution, we can only provide empirical justification for the rank order of individuals on the latent scale—not the distances between them. This is the price we have to pay for not having to specify the prior distribution. But a little reflection will show that this should not surprise us. If our result does not depend on the choice of prior distribution, then it must be true whatever prior we happen to choose. One prior can be transformed into another by stretching or shrinking the latent scale. Such a transformation will leave the rank order unchanged but not the spacing between individuals. Rank order is thus invariant under changes in the prior. In practice it is usual to assume that the prior distribution is normal. There is nothing to prevent us adopting this or whatever other distribution we please, and the spacing that goes with it, so long as we remember that this is a matter of *convention* and not something which has, or can have, empirical support.

All of the foregoing pre-supposes that a model depending on a single latent variable will fit the data. For this to be true, the items must have been expertly constructed to depend on only a one-dimensional scale of ability. For relatively simple skills this may be possible and there are, in fact, many situations where it has been achieved. But with more general abilities, of which 'general intelligence' is the prime, but by no means the only example, this is usually not the case. In such cases the failure to obtain a good fit can best be explained by the presence of other latent variables. Once more than one latent variable is admitted, a new source of arbitrariness arises, which is at the heart of much of the controversy about the validity of the whole approach. We shall illustrate the position by means of an example in Section 6 but it may help at this stage to use an analogy to give some idea of the point at issue.

Position on a map is a two-dimensional thing. We can describe the position of Birmingham as so many miles north of London and so many miles west, using the familiar rectangular co-ordinates. But the choice of north–south and east–west as lines of reference is quite arbitrary. We could have used NE–SW and NW–SE axes. Or we could have specified Birmingham's position in terms of a direction and the distance as the crow flies. All such methods enable us to fix its position but none has any claim on us beyond practical convenience. The existence and position of Birmingham is real enough, but the axes we construct to specify position are merely that—constructs.

If our model fitting exercise tells us that we need two dimensions to describe the latent variation of individuals, we have a similar situation. The variation is real, but to define an individual's location we must construct arbitrary axes with reference to which that location is specified. In a geographical context the north/south axis may have physical significance as, for example, if we wished to specify the positions of the towns on the main east coast railway line between London and Scotland. Similarly a particular axis may have meaning in other contexts but that must not be confused with empirical support.

Once we add a second or further dimension, we may no longer be able to rank individuals. The situation is no different from when we are dealing with observable variables. Suppose candidates A and B take two examination papers, and that A's marks are 87 and 64 and that B's are 76 and 56, then we can say that A is better than B. But if B's marks had been 76 and 65, no such ranking is possible. On Paper I alone A ranks higher, but on Paper II the reverse is true. To arrive at a ranking we have to assign relative weights, explicitly or implicitly, to the two papers, and there is nothing in the data to tell us what those weights should be. Equal weights would put A ahead, but by giving Paper II sufficient weight, B could be made to come out first. A one-dimensional ranking of locations in a many-dimensional space is not, in general, possible. All rankings, such as degree classifications, therefore depend not only on the marks obtained in the examination, but on independent judgements of the weights to be attached to the papers. The same is true of latent variables. We shall illustrate these points by examples in the following sections.

Statistical versus Psychometric Inference

In the psychometrical literature a distinction is drawn between these two kinds of inference. The point at issue can be explained by reference to the array in Table 1. In psychometrical inference the interest is in generalising from the results for the p items selected for the test, to the universe of items which might have been used. The items used are viewed as a sample of the domain of knowledge being examined, and thus subject to uncertainty. The presumption is that we could get nearer to the 'true' ability of each individual if we could increase the number of items indefinitely.

In statistical inference, on the other hand, the n individuals are regarded as a sample from a larger population to which we wish our inferences to apply. The larger the sample size, the more precise will be our information about the characteristics of the items which happen to be included in the test.

In practice both types of generalisation will be of interest, though one or other may be uppermost. For inter-school or regional comparisons, for example, using the same set of items throughout eliminates variation arising from item selection and thus makes school comparisons more efficient. For establishing rank orders within a particular group of individuals, however, what matters is the coverage of the field of knowledge.

Attempts at finding a theoretical basis for psychometrical inference have not been entirely convincing. The root of the difficulty lies in the fact that the domain of items is rarely well-defined and, even if it is, the selection of items is not usually made in a well enough defined way to allow valid generalisations. All that we can do then is to look at the variation among the items that we have selected. For example, if in Table 1 the column totals were identical, we might conclude that all items were equally difficult and hence that the results could be safely generalised. If, on the other hand, there was a good deal of variation in the column totals, we would be less confident that a similar ranking would be obtained among individuals if different items were to be used. All of this pre-supposes that the actual items used are, in some sense, representative. In most cases it is the lack of any information about the sampling process for items which precludes valid inference beyond the set of items to hand.

Although this traditional distinction may be helpful in clarifying our thinking, it is unnecessary in practice. Our modelling approach enables us to make general statements about the latent variables without the need to specify how the items were selected. All that we need to do is specify how those particular scores were generated by the latent variable. This tells us what can be validly said about the latent variable *given* the items which were selected. Equally, if the *n* items are randomly selected from some larger population (real or hypothetical), we can use traditional statistical inference procedures to generalise to that population.

An Example Illustrating Indeterminacies in the Model

So far we have described what a model aims to do and have made some assertions about the practical consequences. These can only be fully justified by mathematical analysis but they can be illustrated by examples to make their implications clearer.

The first example has a long history and was deliberately chosen for that reason. It consists of a test of five items, scored right or wrong, administered to 1000 individuals. It is Section VI of the Law School Admission Test. The left-hand column of Table 2. lists all the 32 possible outcomes of the test ranging from 00000 for someone who gets all items wrong to 11111 for someone who gets them all right. The second column gives the frequencies with which each response pattern occurred. It is immediately obvious that some response patterns are very much more common than others; 173 individuals produced 11011 and only one 00100, for example. Our aim is to try to understand the reasons for this variation and thus to discover what can be inferred about the abilities of the individuals.

We may start with the hypothesis that there is no underlying variation in ability whatsoever. After all it is pointless to enter into debate about scaling ability if the test is no better than a lottery. If this were really the case, all individuals would have the same chance of getting any particular item correct and, let us assume, the chance of getting any item is independent of whether other items were right or wrong. If all of this were true, we can work out what the frequency distribution of response patterns would be. The result is given in column 3 of Table 2. Some are very close to the observed frequencies, but there are also some big discrepancies, most notably where 4 or 5 items are answered correctly. A formal test of agreement confirms that the observed frequency distribution is most unlikely to have arisen from the simple model just described.

Table 2. Observed and expected frequencies for various hypotheses about the distribution of the latent variables for the Law School Admission test Section VI.

Score pattern	Observed frequency	Expected frequencies when:		
		No variation in ability	Two-point distribution	Normal distribution
00000	3	0.3	1.6	2.3
00001	6	2.0	5.6	5.9
00010	2	1.0	2.5	2.6
00011	11	6.6	9.3	8.9
00100	1	0.4	0.7	0.7
00101	1	2.5	2.7	2.6
00110	3	1.2	1.2	1.2
01100	0	0.9	0.9	0.9
00111	4	8.1	5.9	6.0
01000	1	0.7	1.8	1.8
01001	8	5.0	6.7	6.4
01010	0	2.4	3.0	2.9
01011	16	16.0	13.6	13.6
01101	3	6.1	4.3	4.4
01110	2	3.0	2.0	2.0
01111	15	19.8	14.0	13.9
10000	10	3.7	9.4	9.5
10001	29	24.8	35.4	34.6
10010	14	11.9	16.1	15.6
10011	81	79.8	75.5	76.6
10100	3	4.6	4.7	4.7
10101	28	30.7	24.5	25.0
10110	15	14.7	11.2	11.5
10111	80	98.7	84.6	83.5
11000	16	9.0	11.6	11.3
11001	56	60.3	55.3	56.1
11010	21	29.0	25.3	25.7
11011	173	194.4	174.2	173.3
11100	11	11.1	8.3	8.4
11101	61	74.7	63.6	62.5
11110	28	35.9	29.6	29.1
11111	298	240.0	294.8	296.7
Total	1000	999.3	999.9	1000.2

The second model, which is one of those widely used in item response testing, supposes that individuals vary in ability scaled in such a way as to make its distribution normal. In this case the predicted frequencies are as given in the last column of Table 2. The agreement is very much closer, and it may be shown to be well within the limits one would expect if the model were true. This, quite reasonably, has been held to justify regarding the test as measuring variation in the ability needed to pursue a course in law. But that is not the end of the story as the penultimate column in Table 2. shows. This is calculated on the hypothesis that the individuals are divided into two latent groups— what we might call 'high' and 'low' ability groups. A close comparison of the two columns shows that there is hardly anything to choose between them. We can certainly conclude that there is evidence of variation in ability because both models which incorporate this feature do very much better than the one which does not. But when it comes to distinguishing between the radically different patterns of variation in ability which underlie the alternative models, the data give us no practical help!

If we choose to go ahead with the model of continuous normal variation, on the grounds that it is fully consistent with the data, there are further problems. We pointed out that the model enables us to predict an individual's location on the latent scale and to specify our uncertainty about it. The latter can be done in terms of the variance. Prior to observing the test results, the uncertainty may be expressed by the variance of the prior distribution. After we have observed the responses it will be the variance of the posterior distribution that is relevant. In the case of this example, the latter figure is about two thirds of the former. In other words, this particular test has not greatly reduced our uncertainty about where the individual lies. The way to obtain more precise information is to add more items, and theory could guide us on how large the test should be. But the example warns us that a valid test may not be a reliable one.

An Example Illustrating a Two-dimensional Latent Variable

This example relates not to test scores but to the related question of the anxiety people feel about taking tests. It has been chosen because it has been used in many countries (Norway, Germany, Holland, Egypt, India, Hungary, Spain, Korea and Canada), with male and female respondents and with very similar outcomes in all cases. It therefore appears to describe something which is more than an artefact of a particular set of circumstances. We use Canadian data for which further details will be found in Gierl and Rogers (1996). The Test Anxiety Inventory consists of 20 questions about how people feel before taking an examination. They are listed in the Appendix. Individuals respond on a 4-point scale which, for the purposes of this example, are treated as points on a continuous scale. They are usually analysed using a factor model which supposes that the response is a linear combination of one or more latent variables together with an 'error' term. It appears that two latent variables are needed to explain the response patterns and, therefore, that 'test anxiety' is not a one-dimensional phenomenon. This raises the question of how we interpret these dimensions and what reality they have. Some results are given in Table 3.

Readers familiar with factor analysis will recognise that the numbers in this table are *factor loadings*. For our limited purpose here it is sufficient to know that they may be interpreted as correlation coefficients between the item scores and the latent variable supposedly underlying them. Thus in column I of the orthogonal set we notice that all of the correlations with the first latent dimension are positive, mainly large and, for the most part, roughly equal. Since all of the items express anxiety in some form it is natural to identify the dimension with the 'test anxiety' which the items are supposed to be measuring. But that is not the whole story, because there is a second factor represented by

Table 3. Alternative sets of factor loadings for the Test Anxiety Inventory for 389 Canadian female students.

Item	Orthogonal set		Oblique set		Emotional (E) Worry (W)
	I	II	I	II	
1	.64	.04	**.41**	.29	—
10	.55	−.04	**.44**	.15	E
11	.80	−.08	**.66**	.18	E
12	.73	−.05	**.58**	.20	—
13	.61	−.07	**.51**	.13	—
14	.61	.31	.05	**.65**	W
15	.81	−.19	**.74**	.05	E
16	.68	−.24	**.77**	−.07	E
17	.65	.28	.11	**.62**	W
18	.62	−.09	**.54**	.11	E
19	.58	−.37	**.45**	.16	—
2	.72	.07	**.43**	.36	E
20	.66	.22	.20	**.54**	W
3	.46	.26	.01	**.52**	W
4	.62	.18	.22	**.47**	W
5	.49	.35	−.09	**.66**	W
6	.44	.28	−.03	**.54**	W
7	.63	.23	.16	**.55**	W
8	.71	−.22	**.77**	−.04	E
9	.69	−.33	**.89**	−.20	E

column II. This is independent of the first—hence the term orthogonal—and much more weakly related to the observed item scores. The interesting thing is that some of the correlations are positive and some negative. Some help in interpreting this dimension is provided by the last column in which most items are classified as 'worry' and 'emotional' items. The latter are distinguished by the occurrence of autonomous nervous system reactions as, for example in the statement 'While taking examinations I have an uneasy, upset feeling' (item 1). An example of a 'worry' item is 'During exams I find myself thinking about whether I'll ever get through school' (item 5). Four items were not readily classified in either category. For the most part emotional items are negatively correlated with the second latent variable, and the worry items are positively correlated.

The conclusion which emerges from all of this may be expressed as follows. The pattern of responses can be explained by supposing that individuals vary in two dimensions. The dominant dimension can be identified with a generalised kind of anxiety in examination situations of the kind indicated by what is common to the 20 items. But, given any position on this axis, there will be a more limited variation in a direction independent of the first, which distinguishes those where the preponderant aspect is emotional from those for whom it is cognitive.

However, analysts have usually chosen to identify the 'worry' and 'emotional' aspects as the more fundamental. That is they have chosen axes to which individuals are referred which corresponded with these two supposed variables. The results are shown in columns I and II of the 'Oblique set'. According to this representation factor I is the one which, predominantly, correlates with the emotional items (picked out in bold type); factor II correlates with those in the worry category. We then conclude that individuals are characterised by where they stand on those two scales. Unlike those in the Orthogonal set, these latter scales are not independent, but are typically correlated to the degree of about 0.7.

We now have two descriptions (among many others that are possible) of the dimensions of latent variation. One can be generated from the other by a process known technically as rotation. Since there is no empirical means of choosing between these two descriptions it is often argued that neither is real and that it is futile, if not actually harmful, to speak as if there were. This objection misses the point. Both representations describe the same thing but in different ways. Each may be useful in some circumstances but not in others. For example, if our purpose is to understand what makes people anxious about exams, it may be useful to distinguish those feelings which have physical correlates in the functioning of the nervous system from those which do not. If we are more interested in distinguishing those individuals for whom pre-exam anxiety might be an important determinant of performance, it is more useful to know that most of the relevant information is conveyed by dimension I of the orthogonal set. The reality is that individuals differ. The arbitrariness lies in what axes of reference we use to describe those differences.

Group Comparisons

With the advent of league tables of various kinds, comparisons between groups and over time have been at the centre of arguments about the measurement of standards. Because of the public debate on the matter, the problems of interpretation are widely known. The annual dispute about whether improved A-level or GCSE results are due to falling standards or to harder work, better teaching and so forth, serves as a reminder of the issues involved. Here we review these controversies in the light of the modelling approach advocated in this paper.

The essentials can best be exposed by using a little elementary algebra. Suppose that an individual's examination mark on a particular item is denoted by X. We suppose that this depends on how easy the item is, how good the item is for discriminating between people of differing ability, how able the individual is (or how well taught, favourably supported by home environment etc.) and on a multiplicity of minor factors peculiar to the item, the individual and the circumstances. A simple representation of X is then

$$X = E + DA + M.$$

E measures the easiness, and the bigger it is the larger will be X. A is the compound measure we called ability. How much effect this has on X depends on the size of D, the discrimination factor. If the item is good at discriminating, a small change in A will produce a large change in X. Finally, M represents the combined effect of all other factors.

The nub of the difficulty in making comparisons arises from the confounding of D and A and there is no way we can separate the two effects. The usual way out of the impasse is to standardise the distribution of A. We have already noted that this distribution is arbitrary and, as a matter of convention, we can give it any origin and scale that we please. The usual convention is to scale the distribution of A to have zero mean and unit standard deviation. But the very essence of the problem of making comparisons is that the distribution is not the same for the two populations. If we fit the model to data from two groups, any difference in the abilities will show up in the parameters E and D which characterise the items. But if the items are the same, then the difference must be attributed to A. Thus valid comparisons can only be made if the institutions are the same in all other respects. In particular the factors represented by M must be the same. If environmental and other background factors are not the same, this assumption will not be valid. The problem is particularly acute when making comparisons for the same population over time. Performance, or standard, is not the only thing which varies over time, and there is no way the effects can be separated.

All of this is predicated on the supposition that the equation adequately captures the way in which the various factors combine to produce a score. It does not, for example, allow for any interaction between items and institutions. A blatant case of this would occur if one school 'taught for the test' and the other did not, but the effects might be more subtle. All group comparisons must be qualified by the statement 'other things being equal' and in the nature of the case that is a judgement which cannot be tested empirically.

Conclusions and Criticisms

It will be clear that the modelling approach highlights the hazards of attempting to measure standards. Even if a single latent variable is adequate, the most that we can do is to justify a ranking of individuals and, unless the number of items is large, that is likely to be subject to a high degree of uncertainty. When additional latent variables are needed, there is a fundamental arbitrariness in describing the latent space which complicates interpretation. Comparisons between groups or institutions are fraught with difficulties caused by the fact that we cannot separate out all of the factors which contribute to the scores of individuals. This might seem to argue for the abandonment of the enterprise altogether, or reversion to the simple practices which have served for generations. This is to mis-read the situation. The cruder methods do not avoid the difficulties, they merely ignore them. The virtue of the approach we have outlined is that it makes explicit what would otherwise be only implicit. Our intention is constructive not destructive; by showing what is indefensible, the way is cleared to build on a more secure foundation.

There have, however, been criticisms of the whole approach which, if accepted, would leave little intact. These have centred largely on the concept of general intelligence but they apply here also, if with less force. Two eloquent critics are to be found in Gould (1984) and Rose (1997). Neither author is a social scientist nor an expert in measurement theory and their accounts are not wholly reliable. Nevertheless, as popular writers whose work reaches a wide lay audience, it is their interpretation which most people are likely to have encountered.

Each critic seeks to demolish the notion of any real thing called general intelligence using facts which have already come to light in the course of this paper. Rose correctly draws attention to the arbitrariness of the form of the distribution of the latent variable, though it is unclear whether he is actually referring to the latent variable itself, or to some score (such as the sum) derived from the item scores. There is certainly no requirement that this should be normal and the only inferences which are legitimate are those which are independent of the form of the distribution. The main attack of both authors is reserved for the arbitrariness of the axes in the factor space. If different factors can be made to come and go by the whim of the investigator in rotating axes, they cannot be claimed to be 'real'. Spearman's general intelligence vanished when Thurstone rotated the solution to produce a cluster of specific factors. In our example, test anxiety dissolved into two correlated dimensions labelled 'worry' and 'emotional'. The axes we used are, indeed, arbitrary but the space which they span is real in the sense that it is a collective property of the set of items. Whenever several dimensions are needed, no absolute ranking of individuals is possible. It is therefore perfectly legitimate for Rose to point out that different rankings will result from different tests. What matters, however, is relevance for purpose, and we indicated in the test anxiety example how different axes might usefully serve different purposes. A full critique of Rose and Gould is beyond the scope of this paper. Our purpose in raising the matter here is to make clear that nothing they say affects the central argument of this paper. It is variation between individuals which is real; how we describe it is arbitrary but not meaningless.

Appendix

Topics of the 20 test items for the example of Section 6:

1 Lack of confidence during tests

  2 Uneasy, upset feeling
  3 Thinking about grades
  4 Freeze up
  5 Thinking about getting through school
  6 Harder I work, more confused
  7 Thoughts interfere with concentration
  8 Jittery when taking test
  9 Even when prepared, get nervous
10 Uneasy before getting the test back
11 Tense during test
12 Exams bother me
13 Tense/stomach upset
14 Defeat myself during tests
15 Panicky during tests
16 Worry before important tests
17 Think about failing
18 Heart beating fast during tests
19 Can't stop worrying
20 Nervous during tests, forget facts

Discussion

Harvey Goldstein

Introduction

The term 'standard' has come to mean in many educational systems a position on a measurement scale, either ordinal or continuous and presupposes the ability to construct measurements, especially those based around student achievements, along such a scale. Unfortunately, discussions about 'standards' of educational attainment have suffered from the absence of a widely acceptable formal framework. Yet such a framework, with clear definitions and rules for deriving conclusions from stated assumptions, is both desirable and necessary for informed debate. In this paper I shall explore the concept of 'educational standards' and examine the formal assumptions which underlie it.

It appears that the only sustained attempts to provide a formal framework have been those of psychometrics. Yet this discipline has been concerned principally with providing mathematical *models* to describe the responses of subjects (people) to test questions or items, and in particular ways of achieving efficient summaries of those responses. It seems to have been content with establishing a mathematically consistent structure for this special case rather than attempting to formulate a general structure which would allow a wider debate to emerge. For a discussion of some of the limitations of the psychometric approach see Goldstein and Wood (1989). David Bartholomew has provided a succinct discussion of educational measurement and has emphasised the importance and to some extent, arbitrariness, of the assumptions that have to be made in terms of choice of items and populations.

I wish to explore different kinds of frameworks which may be used to characterise notions of educational standards. I start with a definition of a simple formal structure, then describe an alternative approach and finally look at some practical implications. My principal argument is that, without a formal framework, it is extremely difficult to have a useful debate about *measuring* educational standards. The following suggestions are an attempt to provide such a framework in the hope that this will stimulate further debate.

A Simple (Constructionist) Definition

Consider a simple case: we are measuring the attainment of a population for a class of arithmetical operations. Assume that the population is well defined (e.g. all year three children in Welsh schools) and that the class of arithmetical operations is also well defined (e.g. the addition of two 2-digit numbers). Assume also that a suitable sampling procedure is available for the population which will enable an estimate to be made, say of a population mean, with a predetermined accuracy.

In order to provide measurements a procedure is required for constructing a measuring instrument, a test. To construct this test we need to select the items (in the case of the above example there is a finite population of such items), determine how they are presented, administered and the children's responses assessed. Research (see for example Foxman *et al.* 1990) indicates that variations in item format and presentation can affect the proportion of correct responses, so that I shall also assume that these aspects are systematically controlled.[1]

---

[1] Note that other factors such as the ordering of items may affect responses.

Note that other sources of (random) error can arise from the requirements of particular procedures, for example if items are selected from a population of items. Any sampling error produced in such ways can then be incorporated into statements about the precision of estimates.

I shall also suppose that the test constructors have been very careful to carry out a detailed conceptual analysis of what they are trying to measure and that the test and its items have been carefully piloted.

The simple definition is just the population mean of a measuring instrument defined as above. Changes in the standard are measured by the difference in means across populations or across time. A formal definition for this simple case is given in the appendix.

Implications of the Simple Definition

We note that this simple definition implies some important restrictions. First, it requires a very precise operationalisation. Inferences are applicable only to the class of items we have defined. Thus, keeping with our example, if we wish to study 2-digit arithmetic addition when the items are presented in a different fashion, say 'horizontally' rather than 'vertically', then we will need to construct a different test which will then refer to a different 'standard'. This immediately raises the issue of the relationship among such standards. The study of such relationships is then a matter for empirical research and will not be dealt with further in the present paper.

Secondly, it assumes that there is a very clear definition of the population or 'universe' from which the items are selected. In our simple example such a definition seems possible, but in more complex cases, for example in a test of reading comprehension, it may be impossible to define the universe precisely other than in the degenerate case where it consists simply of the single test being used. It is also possible to construct a set of tests and then to make random selections from this set. Such a procedure is similar to those used in conjunction with test equating (see below).

Thirdly, our definition is purely formal. It says nothing about relevance or appropriateness of any test we may construct, nor does it say anything about how a universe of items or a relevant population is to be chosen. As we will argue below, it is just when such choices have to be made that important problems arise which generally cannot be solved by a purely formal procedure.

Applications of the Simple Definition

The simple definition has an obvious application when the same test is used with different populations, usually defined with respect to time (see Start and Wells 1972 for examples). A variant is where a common set of items is used within two or more different tests and the common set forms the basis for inference about population differences.[2]

Problems arise when we wish to make interpretations of any differences: the same kinds of problems arise if we sample from a well defined universe of tests. Start and Wells (1972) show how a reading test used in the late 1940s had changed its interpretation by the 1960s. Language and curriculum usage had changed over the period and the test had become 'harder' as component items became less familiar to the students responding to the test. We may refer to such changing conditions as 'background conditions'. Changes in mean response were observed but it was not felt possible to separate a changing 'test difficulty' from a 'real' population response change.

Over a short period of time, if it is assumed that changes in background conditions are at most negligible, we may draw inferences about standards in terms of the above definition, using either a constant test or one sampled from a suitable universe. Note, however, that we need to make further assumptions, about background conditions, in order to reach conclusions about 'standards'. In the following sections we investigate ways in which changes in such assumptions will affect the inferences which can be made. To introduce this discussion we introduce an underlying philosophical distinction.

Platonic Standards

Most tests, and for that matter examinations, are not constructed using a systematic sampling procedure. Tests are usually constructed by carefully following criteria to do with content, format, relationships with other measurements, tests or items, group differences (biases) and so forth. Empirical piloting and expert assessment may also be applied before a test is used. This procedure may be referred to as 'Platonic' test construction since it relies upon the notion that there exists an 'ideal' underlying test item universe or concept and that the procedures used to

---

[2] For a detailed discussion of such a procedure see Beaton and Zwick (1990). It raises practical difficulties of interpretation, however, since the 'context' of the items differs according to the test within which they are used.

construct a real test are realisations of it. The construction 'rules' are designed to sample from this ideal: unless the concept of such an ideal is invoked the construction rules will be arbitrary. This underlying concept typically will be referred to as 'reading comprehension', 'arithmetic ability', 'understanding of mathematical symmetry' and so on and it is clear that the aim is to make statements about the underlying concept. This Platonic procedure of assuming an underlying concept is different from the constructionist procedure outlined in the first section which formally defines either a particular test or an explicitly constructed universe as the object of inference. Of course, a constructionist procedure may draw upon Platonic notions in order to derive a population in the first place, but thereafter it relies upon clear sampling rules for its operation.

The distinction we are making is more than a philosophical nicety: it has profound implications for the kinds of interpretations that can be made. Consider the above example of the reading test which was assumed to become outdated over time. Once the test had been devised, a strict constructionist interpretation would be indifferent to issues such as 'relevance to curriculum'; all that would be required is that the rules for administering the test to successive populations be adhered to. The additional observation that the test was less relevant in the 1960s can only be admitted if the test itself is just one instance of an underlying reality, which means the adoption of a Platonic viewpoint. Even in the case where the test was used over a short period so that 'relevance' could be assumed to apply, we would still be appealing to this additional assumption of relevance to justify the use of the test.

It would seem that the Platonic view of a test is the one that is very widely adopted, although not universally. The constructionist example we started with, of a well defined arithmetic test, might be regarded as useful if our interest centres on just the universe of items sampled by the test.

One possible objection to the distinction we are making is that the constructionist procedure can be extended to incorporate many of the tests people use without necessarily invoking a Platonic viewpoint. Thus, for example in the reading test case we can envisage a 'super-universe' of items which is constructed by considering the union of the sets of items relevant to all possible populations. If we suppose that it is possible precisely to define a universe for any given population, say of arithmetic or spelling items, then we need merely form the union of these separate universes and sample from this. This presents several difficulties however. First, it does not deal with the example we used to introduce this section, which is very commonly used. Secondly it requires an assumption about the weight to be attached to each item in the super-universe for the purpose of sampling. In general the different populations will have items in common: if we have two populations are the common items to be counted once or twice in the super-universe? Thirdly, if the populations are those chosen at different times, the sampling at the first time can only be made from the universe of items defined at that time—subsequent times are not yet observed and their universes cannot be defined. This introduces an asymmetry which prevents us sampling from the same super-universe at each occasion.

We shall not consider in any more detail the constructionist procedure: the social and political debate on standards rarely is concerned with these. In the following sections we will pursue some of the implications of the Platonic approach.

Platonism in Practice

To understand the implications of a Platonic view of standards, we shall look in a little more detail at that part of mathematics sometimes referred to as 'numeracy' which is largely a subset of elementary arithmetic. Specifically we shall contextualise what we have to say within the political requirement set out by the British Government regarding 'standards of achievement' for Key Stage 2' (eleven year olds) children over the period 1997–2002 (D*f*EE, 1997). This example is chosen because it illustrates the issues in a straightforward fashion and because it has some important contemporary educational implications.

Broadly speaking, attention is focussed on the percentage of children in England and Wales achieving a 'level' 4 in numeracy tests. From a national mean of about 55% in 1997 it is proposed that this should rise to about 80% by the year 2002; several educational programmes have been devised in an attempt to achieve this target. The level for each child, on a scale from 1 to 10, is assigned on the basis of responses to a test, separate tests being devised each year.

It would clearly be possible to adopt a constructionist procedure, whereby an item universe was defined at the outset and sampled from each year. This, however, would appear not to be under consideration and would be difficult to adopt since over several years the definition of the relevant universe would almost certainly change. Rather, the term numeracy is being used in what we have termed a Platonic sense. It is assumed to exist, independently of any specific version of a curriculum, and there are assumed to be more or less well defined procedures for constructing tests which reflect it. Assuming that it does exist, how are we to ensure that our succession of tests reflects it (and no other concept)?

Suppose that we are confronted with different tests at each occasion and that we are not relying upon a common set of items to provide 'continuity', for the reasons outlined above. The possibility of more general 'equating' procedures[3] arises but is not relevant, for the following reason.

The aim of test equating is to allow the scores on two tests, say test A and test B, to be calibrated along the same scale. This may be attempted in a number of ways, but for our purpose suppose that it is done by independently giving each test to each member of a suitably large random sample from a population. Suppose also that the equating 'works' in the sense that each test ranks the sample in a common ordering so that a unique correspondence between test scores can be set up. If we apply such a procedure to two tests at different time points we immediately face the problem of which population is to be used to carry out the equating. If it is the first one, then we require the second test to be available at the time of the first test: this clearly requires that all tests are devised at the outset, which is equivalent to defining a super-universe in the constructionist sense and is anyway practically infeasible. If the standardising population is that at the second occasion then we have a similar problem. Thus, unless we define, as before, a super-universe at the outset, we cannot sample from the later populations at the first time occasion.

In effect, equating attempts to make the same inferences as would be made were the same test to be given at each occasion. Thus, the use of equated tests raises no new fundamental issues beyond those discussed when the same test is used in a constructionist sense. In practice it also introduces further 'noise' since no equating is perfect and there is the problem that the equating calibration relationship may differ across subpopulations of interest (see Goldstein and Wood 1989 for a further discussion).

Having ruled out both simple constructionist and related equating

---

[3] Some kinds of equating procedures, especially those using item response models, are based around such a common item set. Thus they suffer not only from the 'context effect' but also from the problems associated with equating procedures in general (see Goldstein and Wood 1989 for a further discussion).

approaches, what else may be available that allows us to create a series of tests which reflect the concept of numeracy? One procedure would be to invest the responsibility for conforming to a Platonic standard in the hands of a group of individual 'experts' who would use their judgements when creating (and interpreting) tests. Effectively, this is what is done by the British public examination systems where the experts or 'examiners' use a variety of methods, including the study of statistical performance information, to arrive at 'comparability'. It also underlies the various 'standard setting' procedures which are judgementally based (see for example Morrison 1994). It is clear that those involved believe that they are attempting to achieve a correspondence with an underlying or Platonic standard (Cresswell 1997a or b).

An interesting feature of these procedures is that they require a post hoc component. It is not assumed to be possible to create a test or examination, however carefully constructed, that ensures comparability *without* using the empirical evidence obtained from a set of actual responses.[4]

A Basic Limitation of Platonic Standards

Whatever procedure is used to construct a test and to manipulate subsequent scoring or grading systems (a 'testing system'), there is a fundamental problem with the use of a Platonic standard. Any particular testing system will be an approximation to the standard in question. It will be a matter for debate as to how good such an approximation is, and the effort that goes into the construction and scoring is largely devoted to attempting to improve such an approximation.

Nevertheless, *there is no objective way to determine how close any approximation will be.* In particular there is no way of knowing whether the responses to two different testing systems *differ from the standard by the same amount.*[5] In other words any observed difference (apart from

---

[4] It would be possible to obtain a very approximate correspondence to a Platonic standard by removing the post hoc element. This would allow distinctions to be made between 'extreme' performances on the examination and would also allow very crude comparisons over time. In the latter case, however, it would be unable to detect anything other than gross changes.

[5] As in the examination example, it *may* be acceptable to use such approximations for the purpose of detecting 'very large' changes in an underlying standard over time. There remains the problem of defining 'very large' and in practice what is usually required is the detection of moderate change over relatively short periods.

sampling errors) between two populations with separate testing systems will reflect both any underlying difference and the different extent of approximation for each system. This results in an unresolvable duality. Thus, for example, the requirement to detect a given amount of under-lying change, as in the D*f*EE (1997) case, is unrealisable.

This *duality principle* was referred to briefly when discussing the application of a reading test to populations widely separated in time. In that case the debate centred upon the uncertainty about whether the difference between the test and the underlying standard, that is the size of the approximation, had remained constant over time or changed in a particular direction. In effect it was argued that, since the correspon-dence to the school curriculum in particular and to language in general had weakened, so the approximation had become worse. If such an argument is accepted then clearly the test could not be used: there existed no measure of how much the approximation may have changed.[6] As mentioned earlier, only in the simple case where, for example, populations are separated by only a small time difference, may we reasonably assume that the approximations (using the same test) are similar and so attribute even a moderate change in population responses as a change in the underlying standard.

If one accepts the Platonic viewpoint it follows that to make valid comparisons using different measuring instruments it must be demon-strated that the approximations involved have effectively the same magnitude and sign. In doing this one may appeal to the various procedures used and possibly to independent evaluations of them. Any claim about 'standards' then becomes part of a wider concern about the adequacy of the procedures used, and ultimately, perhaps, such a debate may lead to improvements in those procedures.

Comparisons of Educational Systems

There are now many studies involving comparisons of test responses in different countries. This generally involves the same test being used (with translation where appropriate) at a particular time with different educa-tional systems for purposes of comparison. It is not entirely clear whether a constructionist or Platonic view is held by those involved. It

---

[6] In this case, even though a very long time period of over 15 years was involved, the observed differences were not accepted as large enough for a change to be detected given the approx-imations which seemed to be involved.

might seem that a purely constructionist perspective is held in that basic results are typically presented as comparisons of mean scores. In addition, however, it is recognised that responses are related to curriculum content and such relationships are also presented; from such a perspective one might suppose that a Platonic view of different degrees of approximation are assumed to exist. I shall not pursue this further here, but a discussion of some of the most important studies of this kind can be found in an issue of the journal 'Assessment in Education' (Goldstein, H., 1996a).

Implications

My argument may be summarised thus:

1 It is possible to define a constructionist standard for a single test or one derived according to well specified sampling rules. This, by definition, can be used to compare populations and to form (probabilistic) judgements about differences or changes over time. While this approach may be applicable in some circumstances, it appears to be little used in practice.

2 A Platonic standard may be conceptualised, and a testing system can be designed to approximate to it. Such approximation may be adequate for many assessment purposes. When used to measure population *differences*, and in particular changes over time this approach suffers from a fundamental limitation known as the duality principle. This stems from a lack of objective knowledge about the size of the different approximations involved. This limitation precludes the use, in general, of Platonic standards to compare populations unless we can argue convincingly that the approximations used are equivalent in the different populations.

If these points are accepted, then attempts to construct a standard of whatever kind have to confront the difficulties. There appear to be few uncontested examples where a convincing case in favour of a Platonic system has been made. Certainly this case does not seem to be accepted in what is perhaps the most sophisticated large scale system, that of public examinations in Britain.

I have alluded to the possibility that we should restrict comparisons over time, and perhaps across populations, to the detection of gross or extreme changes. In other words we could regard our tests as screening devices for detecting when major changes might be occurring, rather than as precise measurements. Another possibility is to forsake attempts to measure absolute differences in this way and restrict attention to what might be called 'second order' changes, by which I mean the following.

Over time, using a Platonic definition and accepting possibly different degrees of approximation, we can study the relationship between test scores and other factors for each test. Thus, for example, we can examine a gender difference in an attempt to judge whether such a difference had changed between tests. Naturally, we would need to be able to carry out a common standardisation for each test, perhaps simply requiring them to have identical score distributions—this would automatically prevent absolute comparisons but still allow relative, what I have termed second order, comparisons to be made. Such comparisons will be scale dependent and different standardisations may result in different interpretations, but the possibility for potentially useful statements does seem to exist. One might go further and suggest that these second order comparisons are more practically useful than absolute or first order ones since they are an attempt to move closer to causal explanations. Thus, for example, the finding that the difference between girls and boys in examination performance has changed over time (Elwood and Comber, 1996) has generated a debate about possible causes, as well as research into factors which might explain such a change.

Appendix

Formally, denote a specific test for a population as

$$X^{(t)} = \{x_1^{(t)}, x_2^{(t)}, \ldots, x_{n_{(t)}}^{(t)}\}$$

where t denotes the target population, $n_{(t)}$ is the number of items in the test and $x_j^{(t)}$ is the j-th item. Denote $\bar{x}^{(t)}$ by the sample estimate of $\mu^{(t)}$, the required population mean.

The simple definition of a difference in standard between population 1 and population 2 is $\mu^{(1)} - \mu^{(2)}$. These populations may be two 'real' populations (for example Wales and Scotland) or the same geographically defined population at different times (for example Wales in 1970 and 1990). Typically we shall be considering the latter case. Using sample estimates we wish to make a statement about $\mu^{(1)} - \mu^{(2)}$, for example to provide a confidence interval.

We can extend our reasoning to any population parameter, for example the median, without alteration. We can also extend our reasoning to *any* well defined procedure for eliciting responses, for example based upon detailed observations or the administration of practical tasks.

Ian Plewis

The 1988 Education Reform Act led to a system of national assessment, with compulsory assessment for pupils in state-funded schools at the ages of seven, eleven and fourteen. More recently, so-called baseline assessment has been introduced for pupils in their first term of the reception year although the instruments used are not uniform across Local Education Authorities. The nature and purposes of national assessment have changed over the last decade but, throughout, there has been less interest in accurately ranking individual pupils than is the case for public examinations at ages sixteen and eighteen. Important as the outcomes of the national assessments are for pupils and their parents, they do not affect pupils' life chances in the same way as GCSEs and A-levels do. The agenda is, therefore, increasingly driven by what Bartholomew refers to in section seven of his paper as 'aggregate' comparisons. And, as his and earlier papers make clear, it is very difficult, if not impossible, to make the comparisons which politicians are demanding from the system of national assessment which they created.

There are, in principle, at least five kinds of comparisons for which a system of national assessment might be used:

a comparisons between schools;

b comparisons over time or between cohorts of pupils;

c comparisons between different subject areas;

d comparisons of the performance of different socio-economic and demographic groups;

e comparisons over age or developmental changes.

The first two of these are the ones favoured by politicians. Comparisons between schools in the form of rankings, or league tables, are, despite their popularity with some politicians, now widely recognised to be fatally flawed (see, for example, Goldstein 1999). Analysing differences between schools can, however, form the basis of a useful research agenda.

As Bartholomew points out, comparisons over time rest on dubious assumptions. These seem likely to become increasingly untenable as the stakes attached to results at Key Stages One and Two become higher so that teachers teach to the test more and more. There are also, as Plewis (1999) points out, problems when it comes to assessing performance in different subject areas.

Comparisons of the performance of pupils in different socio-economic groups have received rather little attention, with the possible exception of gender differences. However, if we are prepared to make some assumptions, and ultimately all comparisons rest on assumptions which are often to difficult to test, then some progress can be made. In terms of the equation on page 135:

$$X = E + DA + M$$

then, if we assume that E (easiness), D (discrimination) and M (other factors) do not vary across groups, then we can, in principle, look at inequalities. Moreover, if we assume that changes in E, D and M are uniform across groups then we can look at how inequalities are changing. It is important to remember, as Plewis (1998) points out, that overall improvements over time in the proportions of pupils reaching, say, level four at Key Stage Two can be consistent with increasing inequalities.

In many ways, changes with age—or developmental changes—are the changes most closely related to learning and might, therefore, feature more strongly in debates than they do at present. The methodological challenges of constructing a scale applicable over the ages five to sixteen, so that changes with age can be measured, are considerable. On the other hand, this is a potential strength of the ten point scale currently in use. Unfortunately, the absence of any concerted research on the properties of the ten point scale is regrettable. To return to my earlier point about the differences between the purposes and organisation of assessment systems, the public examination system is run on essentially market principles and yet, despite the wish to protect commercial secrets, there is, ironically, more methodological research published from the exam boards than there is from the quango which is the Qualifications and Curriculum Authority (QCA). Perhaps such research is seen as abstruse and irrelevant to policy and the practice of teaching but its absence throughout the decade of national assessment is surely a national scandal.

Bibliography

Adams, J. (1912). *The Evolution of Educational Theory* (London, Macmillan).

AIE (1996). *Assessment in Education*, **3**(2).

Aldrich, R. (1995). *School and Society in Victorian Britain: Joseph Payne and the new world of education* (New York, Garland).

Aldrich, R. (1996). *Education for the Nation* (London, Cassell).

Aldrich, R. (1997). *The End of History and the Beginning of Education* (London, Institute of Education).

Aldrich, V. C. (1963). *Philosophy of Art* (Englewood Cliffs, Prentice-Hall).

Anderson, R. D. (1995). *Education and the Scottish People* (Oxford, Oxford University Press).

Arnold, Matthew (1863). *A French Eton*, reprinted in *The Complete Prose Works of Matthew Arnold vol. ii, Democratic Education* ed. R. H. Super (Ann Arbor, University of Michigan Press, 1962), pp 262–325.

Arnott, M. (1993). Thatcherism in Scotland: an Exploration of Educational Policy in the Secondary Sector (PhD Thesis, Strathclyde University).

Ayer, A. J. (1946). *Language Truth and Logic* Second edition (London; Penguin).

Baird, J. (1998). What's in a Name? Experiments with blind marking in A-level Examinations. *Educational Research*, **40**(2), 191–202.

Baird, J. and Jones, B. (1998). Statistical analyses of examination standards: better measures of the unquantifiable? (Associated Examining Board Research Report—RAC/780).

Bardell, G.; Fearnley, A. and Fowles, D. (1984). *The contribution of graded objectives schemes in Mathematics and French* (Manchester, Joint Matriculation Board).

Barnes, B. (1974). *Scientific Knowledge and Sociological Theory* (London, Routledge and Kegan Paul).

Bartholomew, D. J. and Knott, M. (1999). *Latent Variable Models and Factor Analysis* (2nd edition) (London, Arnold).

Bartholomew, D. J. (1996). *The Statistical Approach to Social Measurement* (San Diego, Academic Press).

Beardsley, M. C. (1981). *Aesthetics: Problems in the Philosophy of Criticism* (Indianapolis, Hackett).

Beaton, A. E. and Zwik, R. (1990). *Disentangling the NAEP 1985–86 reading anomaly.* (Princeton, Educational Testing Service).

Benn, C. and Chitty, C. (1996). *Thirty Years On* (London, David Fulton).

Berger, P. and Luckmann, T. (1966). *The Social Construction of Reality* (London, Penguin).

Berry, C. (1997). *Social Theory of the Scottish Enlightenment* (Edinburgh, Edinburgh University Press).

Best, D. (1985). *Feeling and Reason in the Arts* (London, Allen & Unwin).

Bierhoff, H. (1996). Laying the foundation of numeracy: a comparison of primary school textbooks in Britain, Germany and Switzerland. *Teaching Mathematics and Its Applications*, **15**, 141–60.

Billington, R. (1988). *Living Philosophy: An Introduction to Moral Thought* (London, Routledge).

Bourdieu, P. (1989). *La Noblesse d'État: Grandes Écoles et Esprit de Corps* (Paris, Les Editions de Minuit).

Brock, M.G. and Curthoys, M.C. (1998). (eds.). *The History of the University of Oxford vol. vi, Nineteenth-Century Oxford, Part 1* (Oxford, Clarendon Press).

Brooks, G. (1997). Trends in standards of literacy in the United Kingdom, 1948–1996 (paper presented at the UK Reading Association conference, University of Manchester, July 1997, and at the British Educational Research Association conference, University of York, September 1997).

Brown, A., McCrone, D., Paterson, L. and Surridge, P. (1998). *The Scottish Electorate* (London, Macmillan).

Burnhill, P., Garner, C. and McPherson, A. (1990). Parental education, social class and entry to higher education, 1976–1986. *Journal of the Royal Statistical Society*, series A, **153**, 233–248.

Burstein, J., Kaplan, R., Wolff, S., and Chi, L. (1997). Using Lexical Semantic Techniques to Classify Free-Responses (Princeton N.J. Educational Testing Service Research Report available on ETSnet at http: //www.ets.org/research/siglex.html).

Christie, T. and Forrest, G. M. (1981). *Defining Public Examination Standards* (London, Schools Council/Macmillan).

Cipolla, C. M. (1969). *Literacy and Development in the West* (London, Penguin).

Clanchy, M. (1979). *From Memory to Written Record: England 1066–1307* (London, Edward Arnold).

Collins, R. (1979). *The Credential Society* (New York, Academic Press).

Committee of Council on Education (1863). *Report of the Committee of Council on Education 1862–63* (London).

Committee of Council on Education (1872). *Report of the Committee of Council on Education 1871–72* (London).

Committee of Council on Education (1873). *Report of the Committee of Council on Education 1872–73* (London).

Committee of Council on Education (1883). *Report of the Committee of Council on Education 1882–83* (London).

Copeland, J. (1993). *Artificial Intelligence: A Philosophical Introduction* (Oxford, Blackwell).

Cox, C. B. and Dyson, A. E. (1971). (eds.). *The Black Papers on Education* (London, Davis-Poynter).

Cresswell, M. J. (1987). Describing Examination Performance: grade criteria in public examinations. *Educational Studies*, **13**(3), 247–65.

Cresswell, M. J. (1990). Gender Effects in GCSE — Some Initial Analyses (Paper prepared for a Nuffield Seminar at University of London Institute of Education on 29 June 1990) (Unpublished Associated Examining Board Research Report — RAC/517).

Cresswell, M. J. (1994). Aggregation and Awarding methods for National Curriculum

Assessments in England and Wales: a comparison of approaches proposed for Key Stages 3 and 4. *Assessment in Education*, **1**(1), 45–61.

Cresswell, M. J. (1995). Technical and Educational Implications of using Public Examinations for Selection to Higher Education. In T. Kellaghan (ed.), *Admission to Higher Education: Issues and Practice* (Dublin, Educational Research Centre and Princeton, International Association for Educational Assessment).

Cresswell, M. J. (1996). Defining, Setting and Maintaining Standards in Curriculum Embedded Examinations: Judgemental and Statistical Approaches. In H. Goldstein and T. Lewis (eds.). *Assessment: Problems, Developments and Statistical Issues* (London, Wiley).

Cresswell, M. J. (1997a). *Examining Judgements: Theory and Practice of Awarding Public Examination Grades* (PhD thesis, University of London Institute of Education).

Cresswell, M. J. (1997b). Can Examination Grade Awarding be Objective and Fair at the Same Time? Another Shot at the Notion of Objective Standards (Unpublished Associated Examining Board Research Report — RAC/733).

Cresswell, M. J. and Houston, J. G. (1991). Assessment of the National Curriculum — some fundamental considerations. *Educational Review.* **43**, 63–78.

Cressy, D. (1980). *Literacy and the Social Order: reading and writing in Tudor and Stuart England* (Cambridge, Cambridge University Press).

Damasio, A. R. (1995). *Descartes Error: Emotion, Reason and the Human Brain* (London, Papermac).

Davis, E. (1993). *Schools and the State* (London, Social Market Foundation).

Dean, C. (1998). Standards are not parents' top priority. *Times Educational Supplement*, 9 October.

Dearing, R. (1995). *Review of the 16–19 qualifications* (London, Department of Education).

Dennett, D. (1993). *Consciousness Explained* (London, Penguin).

Department for Education and Employment (DfEE). (1997). *Excellence in Schools* (London, Stationery Office).

Department of Education and Science (1967). *Children and Their Primary Schools. A Report of the Central Advisory Council for Education (England).* ii (London, DES).

Devine, M., Hall, J., Mapp, J. and Musselbrook, K. (1996). *Maintaining Standards: Performance at Higher Grade in Biology, English, Geography and Mathematics* (Edinburgh, Scottish Council for Research in Education).

Devlin, K. (1997). *Goodbye Descartes: The End of Logic and the Search for a New Cosmology of the Mind* (New York, Wiley).

Dore, R. (1996). *The Diploma Disease.* 2nd edition (London, Institute of Education).

Dreyfus, H. L. (1992). *What computers still can't do: a critique of artificial reason.* (Cambridge Mass., MIT Press).

Eagleton, T. (1993). *Literary Theory: An Introduction* (Oxford, Blackwell).

Eiser, J. R. (1990). *Social Judgement* (Milton Keynes, Open University Press).

Elwood, J. and Comber, C. (1996). *Gender differences in examinations at 18+* (London, Institute of Education).

Firestone, W. A. (1998). A Tale of Two Tests: Tensions in Assessment Policy. *Assessment in Education*, **5**(2), 175–192.

Fletcher, S. (1980). *Feminists and Bureaucrats. A study in the development of girls' education in the nineteenth century* (Cambridge, Cambridge University Press).

Fogelin, R. J. (1967). *Evidence and Meaning: Studies in Analytic Philosophy* (London, Routledge).

Forrest, G. M. and Orr, L (1984). *Grade Characteristics in English and Physics* (Manchester;,Joint Matriculation Board).

Foxman, D., Ruddock, G. and McCallum, I. (1990). *APU mathematics monitoring 1984–88 (Phase 2)* (London, Schools Examination and Assessment Council).

Fremer, J. (1989). Testing Companies, Trends and Policy Issues: A current view from the testing industry. In B. R. Gifford (ed.), *Test Policy and the Politics of Opportunity Allocation: The Workplace and the Law* (Boston, Kluwer).

French, S., Slater, J. B., Vassiloglou, M. and Willmott, A. S. (1987). *Descriptive and Normative Techniques in Examination Assessment* (Oxford, UODLE).

Galton, M. (1998). Back to consulting the ORACLE. *Times Educational Supplement*, 3 July.

Gierl, M. J. and Rogers, W. J. (1996). Factor analysis of the Test Anxiety Inventory using Canadian high school students. *Educational and Psychological Measurement*, **56**, 315–324.

Goldstein, H. (1983). Measuring Changes in Educational Attainment Over Time: Problems and Possibilities. *Journal of Educational Measurement*, **20**, 369–78.

Goldstein, H. (1995). *Interpreting International Comparisons of Student Achievement* (Paris, UNESCO).

Goldstein, H. (1996a) (ed.). *Assessment in Education, 3*, 2. Special Issue: The IEA Studies.

Goldstein, H. (1996b). International Comparisons of Student Achievement. In Little and Wolf (1996).

Goldstein, H. (1999). Performance Indicators in Education. In D. Dorling and S. Simpson (eds.). *Statistics in Society* (London, Arnold).

Goldstein, H. and Cresswell, M. J. (1996). The comparability of different subjects in public examinations: a theoretical and practical critique. *Oxford Review of Education*, **22**(4), 435–42.

Goldstein, H. and Wood, R. (1989). Five decades of item response modelling. *British Journal of Mathematical and Statistical Psychology*, **42**, 139–167.

Good, F. J. and Cresswell, M. J. (1988a). *Grading the GCSE* (London, Secondary Examinations Council).

Good, F. J. and Cresswell, M. J. (1988b). *Differentiated Assessment: Grading and Related Issues* (London, Secondary Examinations Council).

Gould, S.J. (1984). *The Mismeasure of Man* (London, Penguin).

Gray, J., Hopkins, D., Reynolds, D., Wilcox, B., Farrell, S. and Jesson, D. (1999). *Improving Schools: Performance and Potential* (Milton Keynes, Open University Press).

Gray, J., McPherson, A. and Raffe, D. (1983). *Reconstructions of Secondary Education* (London, Routledge).

Green, A., Leney, T. and Wolf, A. (1997). *Convergences and Divergences in European Education and Training Systems* (Brussels, EC Directorate-General XXII (Education, Training and Youth)).

Green, A., Wolf, A. and Leney, T. (1999). *Convergence and Divergence in European Education and Training Systems* (London, Institute of Education).

Hacking, I. (1965). *The Logic of Statistical Inference* (Cambridge, Cambridge University Press).

Hacking, I. (1990). *The Taming of Chance* (Cambridge, Cambridge University Press).

Hambleton, R. K. and Zaal, J. N. (eds.) (1991). *Advances in Educational and Psychological Testing* (Boston, Kluwer).

Hargreaves, D. H. (1996). Teaching as a research-based profession: policies and prospects (Teacher Training Agency annual lecture).

Heath, A. F. and Clifford, P. (1990). Class inequalities in education in the twentieth century. *Journal of the Royal Statistical Society*, series A, **153**, 1–16. .

Holland, P. W. and Rubin, D. B. (1982). *Test Equating* (New York, Academic Press).

Hollis, M. and Lukes, S. (1982). (eds). *Rationality and Relativism* (Oxford, Blackwell).

Holmes, E. (1911). *What Is and What Might Be* (London, Constable).

Jencks, C. (1972). *Inequality: A Reassessment of the Effect of Family and Schooling in America* (New York, Basic Books).

Johnson, V. E. (1997). An alternative to the traditional GPA for evaluating student performances. *Statistical Science*, **12**, 251–278.

Kelly, A. (1976). A study of the comparability of external examinations in different subjects. *Research in Education*, **16**, 37–63.

Kilpatrick, J. and Johansson, B. (1994). Standardised Mathematics Testing in Sweden: The Legacy of Frits Wigforss. *Nordic Studies in Mathematics Education*, **1**, 6–30.

Koretz, D., Broadfoot, P. and Wolf, A. (1998) (eds.). *Assessment in Education*, **5**(3) (Special Issue on Portfolios and Records of Achievement).

Kuhn, T. (1970). *The Structure of Scientific Revolutions*, second edition (Chicago, University of Chicago Press).

Lakatos, I. (1974). *Proofs and Refutations: the Logic of Mathematical Discovery* (Cambridge, Cambridge University Press).

Little, A. (1996) (ed.). *Assessment in Education*, **4**(1) (Special Issue: The Diploma Disease Twenty Years On).

Little, A., Wang Gang, and Wolf, A. (1995) (eds.). *Sino-British Perspectives on Educational Assessment* (London, ICRA, Institute of Education).

Little, A. and Wolf, A. (1996) (eds.). *Assessment in Transition: Learning, monitoring and selection in international perspective* (Oxford, Pergamon).

Long, H. A. (1985). Experience of the Scottish Examinations Board in developing a grade-related criteria system of awards (Paper presented at the 11th annual conference of the International Association for Educational Assessment held in Oxford, England).

Macaulay, Lord (1898). *Collected Works*, 12 vols. (London, Longmans Green).

Mackenzie, D. A. (1981). *Statistics in Britain 1865–1930. The Social Construction of Scientific Knowledge* (Edinburgh, Edinburgh University Press).

McKenzie, D. (1994). The irony of educational review. *New Zealand Annual Review of Education*, **4**, 247–59.

McLean, L. D. (1996). Large-Scale Assessment Programmes in Different Countries and International Comparisons. In H. Goldstein and T. Lewis (eds.), *Assessment: Problems, Developments and Statistical Issues* (Chichester, Wiley).

McPherson, A. and Willms, J. D. (1987). Equalisation and improvement: some effects of comprehensive reorganisation in Scotland. *Sociology*, **21**, 509–39.

Madaus, G. and Raczek, A. (1996). Turning Point for Assessment: Reform Movements in the United States. In Little and Wolf (1996).

Menet, J. (1874). *A Letter to a Friend on the Standards of the New Code of the Education Department* (London, Rivingtons).

Morrison, H. G., Busch, J. C. and D'arcy, J. (1994). Setting reliable national curriculum standards: a guide to the Angoff procedure. *Assessment in Education*, **1**, 181–199.

Murphy, R. J. L. (1982). Sex differences in Objective Test performance. *British Journal of Educational Psychology*, **52**, 213–19.

Murphy, R. J. L., Burke, P., Cotton, T., Hancock, J., Partington, J., Robinson, C., Tolley, H., Wilmut, J. and Gower, R. (1996). *The Dynamics of GCSE Awarding: Report of a project conducted for the School Curriculum and Assessment Authority* (London, SCAA).

Newcastle Report (1861). *Report of the Commissioners appointed to inquire into the State of Popular Education in England*, PP 1861 XXI (ii) (London).

Newton, P. (1996). The reliability of marking of GCSE scripts: Mathematics and English. *British Educational Research Journal*, **22**, 405–20.

Newton, P. (1997a). Measuring comparability of standards between subjects: why our statistical techniques do not make the grade. *British Educational Research Journal*, **23**(4), 433–49.

Newton, P. (1997b). Examining Standards Over Time *Research Papers in Education*, **12**(3), 227–48.

Orr, L. and Forrest, G. M. (1984). *Investigation into the relationship between grades and assessment objectives in History and English examinations* (Manchester, Joint Matriculation Board).

Orr, L. and Nuttall, D. L. (1983). *Determining Standards in the Proposed Single System of Examinations at 16+* (London, Schools Council).

Paterson, L. (1992). The influence of opportunity on aspirations among prospective university entrants from Scottish schools, 1970–1988. *Statistics in Society, Journal of the Royal Statistical Society*, series A, **155**, 37–60.

Paterson, L. (1995). Social origins of under-achievement among school-leavers. In L. Dawtrey, J. Holland, M. Hammer and S. Sheldon (eds.), *Equality and Inequality in Education Policy* (Milton Keynes, Open University Press).

Paterson, L. (1997). Student achievement and educational change in Scotland, 1980–1995. *Scottish Educational Review*, **29**, 10–19.

Paterson, L. (1998). The Scottish parliament and Scottish civil society: which side will education be on? *Political Quarterly*, **69**, 224–33.

Paterson, L. (forthcoming). Scottish traditions in education. In H. Holmes (ed.), *Compendium of Scottish Ethnology, vol. 11* (Edinburgh, Scottish Ethnological Research Centre).

Paterson, L. and Raffe, D. (1995). Staying on in full-time education in Scotland. *Oxford Review of Education*, **21**, 3–23.

Payne, J. (1872). 'Why are the Results of our Primary Instruction so Unsatisfactory?', *Transactions of the National Association for the Promotion of Social Science.*

Phillips, M. (1996). *All Must Have Prizes* (London, Little, Brown and Company).

Pirsig, R. M. (1974). *Zen and the Art of Motorcycle Maintenance: An Inquiry into Values* (London, Bodley Head).

Plewis, I. (1998). Inequalities, Targets and Zones. *New Economy*, **5**, 104–8.

Plewis, I. (1999). What's Worth Comparing in Education? In D. Dorling and S. Simpson (eds.). *Statistics in Society* (London, Arnold), 273–80.

Pole, D. (1961). *Conditions of Rational Inquiry: A Study in the Philosophy of Value* (London, Athlone).

Power, M. (1997). *The Audit Society: Rituals of Verification* (Oxford, Oxford University Press).

QCA (1998). *GCSE and GCE A/AS code of practice* (London, Qualifications and Curriculum Authority).

Reynolds, D., Creemers, B. P. M., Stringfield, S. and Teddlie, C. (1998). Climbing an educational mountain: conducting the International School Effectiveness Research Project. In G. Walford, *Doing research about education* (Lewes, Falmer Press).

Roach, J. P. C. (1971). *Public Examinations in England 1850–1900* (Cambridge, Cambridge University Press).

Robertson, C. (1992). Routes to higher education in Scotland. *Scottish Educational Review*, **24**: 3–16.

Rose, S. (1997). *Lifelines, Biology, Freedom, Determinism* (London, Penguin).

Sadler, D. R. (1987). Specifying and promulgating achievement standards. *Oxford Review of Education*, **13**, 191–209.

Schools Council (1979). *Standards in Public Examinations: Problems and Possibilities*, Report from the Schools Council Forum on Comparability (London, Schools Council).

SEC (1984). *The development of Grade-related Criteria for the General Certificate of Secondary Education—a briefing paper for working parties* (London, Secondary Examinations Council).

SEC (1985). *Reports of the Grade-related Criteria Working Parties* (London, Secondary Examinations Council).

SEC (1986). Draft Grade Criteria. *SEC News Number 2* (London, Secondary Examinations Council).

SEC (1987). Grade Criteria—Progress Report. *SEC News Number 6* (London, Secondary Examinations Council).

Shavit, Y. and Blossfeld, H. P. (1993). *Persistent Inequality: Changing Educational Attainment in Thirteen Countries* (Boulder, Col., Westview Press).

Skolöverstyrelsen (1980). Quoted in J. Kilpatrick and B. Johansson (1994). Standardised Mathematics Testing in Sweden: The legacy of Frits Wigforss. *Nordic Studies in Mathematics Education*, **1**, 6–30. .

Smith, J. V. and Hamilton, D. (1980) (eds). *The Meritocratic Intellect* (Aberdeen, Aberdeen University Press).

Start, B. and Wells, K. (1972). *The trend of reading standards* (Slough, National Foundation for Educational Research).

Stedman, L. C. (1998). An Assessment of the Contemporary Debate over US

Achievement. In D. Ravitch (ed.), *Brookings Papers on Education Policy* (Washington DC, Brookings Institution Press), 53–119.

Stephens, W. B. (1987). *Education, Literacy and Society, 1830–70: the geography of diversity in provincial England* (Manchester, Manchester University Press).

Sutherland, G. (1973a). *Policy-Making in Elementary Education 1870–1895* (Oxford, Clarendon Press).

Sutherland, G. (1973b) (ed.). *Matthew Arnold on Education* (London, Penguin).

Sutherland, G. (1984). *Ability, Merit and Measurement. Mental testing and English education 1880–1940* (Oxford, Clarendon Press).

The Scotsman Education (1998). 30 September: 4–5.

Thom, D. (1986). The 1944 Education Act: the 'art of the possible. In Harold L. Smith (ed.), *War and Social Change: British Society in the Second World War* (Manchester, Manchester University Press), 101–28.

Vincent, D. (1989). *Literacy and Popular Culture: England 1750–1914* (Cambridge, Cambridge University Press).

Walden, G. (1996). *We Should Know Better: solving the educational crisis* (London, Fourth Estate).

Wang Binhua (1995). Comparing HSCE in the People's Republic of China and GCSE in England. In Little, Wolf and Wang Gang (1995).

Wang Gang (1995). The Development of Public Educational Examinations in China from 1980. in Little, Wolf and Wang Gang (1995).

Wiliam, D. (1996a). Meanings and Consequences in Standard Setting. *Assessment in Education*, 3(3), 287–307.

Wiliam, D. (1996b). Standards in examinations: a matter of trust? *The Curriculum Journal*, 7(3), 293–306.

Wilmut, J. and Rose, J. (1989). *The Modular TVEI Scheme in Somerset: its concept, delivery and administration* (Report to the Training Agency of the Department of Employment, London).

Wolf, A. (1995). Competence Based Assessment (Buckingham, Open University Press).

Wolf, A. and Steedman, H. (1998). Basic Competence in Mathematics: Swedish and English 16 year olds. *Comparative Education*, **34**, 3.

Wood, R. (1991). *Assessment and Testing: A survey of research* (Cambridge, Cambridge University Press).

Young, M. (1958). *The Rise of the Meritocracy 1870–2033* (London, Penguin).